Understanding the Power of Covenants

By

Dr. Mary J. Ogenaarekhua

Endorsements

*"In **Understanding the Power of Covenants**, Dr. Mary J. Ogenaarekhua leads us in both a literal and spiritual journey from 'covenant defined' to 'covenant applied,' and she has strategically designed it to enhance our covenant relationships and benefits in God. **Proverbs 4:7** says that 'wisdom is the principal thing, therefore, get wisdom; and with all thy getting, get understanding!' I believe that everyone who reads this book can expect to receive wisdom and understanding of the power and purpose of God's inspired covenants in ourlives."*

—**Dr. Belinda Campbell, Founder and Teacher,**
World in Prayer Ministries, Inc., Atlanta, Georgia.

*"Covenants! Covenants! Covenants! How many did you make today? Every agreement you make, every hand you shake, and every promise you speak is a form of covenant. Find out how covenants have been impacting your life in this revealing look of how we make and invoking covenants that either prosper or hinder ourlives. Dr. Mary Ogenaarekhua's **Understanding the Power of Covenants**, empowers you to remove the devil's legalities and technicalities (open doors) that he has been using against you and to apply the covenants that move the hand of God in your life."*

—**Lynne Garbinsky, Chief Operations Officer,**
THGP/MJM, Atlanta, Georgia.

Dedication

As in my other books, I dedicate this book to God the Father, God the Son and God the Holy Ghost. Lord God, You gave me the words to write in this book and I give you all the glory. As it is written in **Psalm 68:11**, so You have done concerning this book:

> *"The Lord gave the word: great was the company of those that published it."*

Thanks Father for teaching me the power of covenants and how to use them effectively in my life. Thanks for also helping me to understand how You use covenants and how the devil uses covenant agreements to hinder and destroy people's lives. It is a great honor to have You as my Father and teacher. May this book open the eyes of many and bring deliverance to those that have been hindered by negative covenants in their lives. You are the best Father and teacher and I love You.

Again, I thank You for giving me **To His Glory Publishing Company**. You have made it a great company. Father, to You be all the glory in Jesus name.

Understanding the Power of Covenants

Unless otherwise indicated, all scriptures are quoted from the King James and the New International Versions of the Bible.

Published by: **To His Glory Publishing Company, Inc.**
463 Dogwood Drive, NW
Lilburn, GA 30047
(770) 458-7947
www.tohisglorypublishing.com
www.maryjministries.org

Copyright **2008**© Mary J. Ogenaarekhua. All rights reserved. No part of this book may be reproduced or retransmitted in any form or by any means without the written permission of the author or the publisher.

Book is available at:
Amazon.com, BarnesandNoble.com, Borders.com, Booksamillion. com, etc.
Book is also available in UK and Canada

www.tohisglorypublishing.com
(770) 458-7947

ISBN: 978-0-9791566-8-7   or   0-9791566-8-8

Table of Contents

Preface 13
Acknowledgments 15

Chapter 1:
The Power of Covenants 17
Covenant Defined 17
How to Recognize an Evil Covenant 18
The Power of the Abrahamic Covenant in Our Lives Today 18
The Consequences of Violating the Abrahamic Covenant 22
God's Covenant with the Children of Israel 24
The Everlasting Covenant that the Lord Jesus Established 28
Judas Betrayal of a Covenant Brother 30
Covenant Benefits and Position in the Kingdom of God 32
God Wants a Being that He Can Relate To 35
All Believers Have the Mark of Jesus on Their Foreheads 37
Making an Evil Covenant 40
Examples of Evil Covenants in My Life 40
The Power and Effect of the Ungodly Words of a Parent 46
The Ungodly Covenant by the Children of Israel 50
How God Views the Marriage Covenant 53
The Future Fate of Covenant Breakers 55
Understanding How God's Kingdom is Set Up 56

Chapter 2:
Understanding How God Uses Covenants 61
Divine Presence 68
Divine Protection 71
Divine Empowerment 73
Divine Provision 79
Divine Healing 80
The Bond Slave Covenant 82
Our Duties 87
A Look at How God Uses Covenant 90
How to Put God in Remembrance of His Covenant 100

Prayer to Renounce Wrong Covenants 103

Chapter 3:
Overcoming the Devil's Legalities & Technicalities 107
Our Words 111
Our Beliefs 116
What We See and Dream 117
    1. God Is the First Source of Your Visions and Dreams 119
    2. The Devil Is the Second Source of Your Visions and Dreams 122
    3. You Are the Third Source of Your Visions and Dreams 123
        Partnership or Association 124
Vision Killers 129
An Experience with a Jealous "Friend" 130
Example of How the Devil Hinders with a Covenant 133
    1. A Vision of the Spirits of Hindrances 134

Chapter 4:
Walking in the Path of Safety 143
Do Not Go Around the Mountain Again 143
God's Wrestling with New Believers 145
Why the Wilderness? 146
God Wants to Know How Deep Your Love Is 148
Learning God's Priority 150
The Importance of the Fear of the Lord 151
Understanding the Need for Holiness 167
The Highway of Safety 169
Seven Privileges of Being on the Path of Safety 171
    1. God's Friend and Confidant 171
    2. You Receive the Ability to Discern God's Voice 173
    3. Your Path Becomes a Shining Light 175
    4. You Can Change and Defeat the Enemy's Plans 177
    5. Evil Reports Will Not Move You 180
    6. You Will Know the Benefit of Dying to Self 181
    7. Prayer to Ask the Lord to Set You On the Path of Safety 183

Seven Things that Will Keep You in the Path of Safety 184
    1. Walk in Meekness 184
    2. Walk in Love and Be a Covenant Keeper 185
    3. Have Integrity 185
    4. Keep Thy Lips from Speaking Guile 186
    5. Depart from Evil and Do Good 187
    6. Avoid Iniquities and Walk in the Fear of the Lord 187
    7. Let the Lord Be Your Light 192

Conclusion 197
Bibliography 201

Preface

Many people do not understand why they cannot get out of a cycle of affliction, poverty, unmarriedness, mental diseases, unemployment and many other things that the devil has been using to make their lives miserable. God created us for His abundance, His love, His prosperity and His joy but very many people have lived and died in miserable conditions and many of their children grow up only to be caught in similar situations. This is one of the reasons why when you look at some families, the males tend to die young, the women get pregnant in their teens and never get married, there is unemployment, imprisonment, generational curses of sickness and diseases, etc. If this has been the story of your life, of your family or of some people that you know, be aware that it is not God's plan for people to live all their lives in misery, poverty, ill-health, lack, agony and die without tasting His abundance.

There is an entity out there that hates every human being and many people have not been able to identify how he has been able to defeat every generation in their family and how he has been able to bring them to despair, misery and ruin in every stage of their lives. One of the reasons is because many do not understand the power of covenants. A covenant is a legally binding agreement spiritually and physically and those who do not understand how God uses covenants will continue to live their lives short of the abundance and joy that God has for them. Also, those who do not understand how the devil uses covenants will continue to be his victims unintentionally.

I believe that every human being needs to learn what covenants are and needs to understand how God and the devil uses covenants in human lives. Therefore, this book is intended to open the spiritual eyes of the reader so that he or she can reclaim those things that the devil stole from him or her and from the generations that had gone before. Understanding the power of covenant will change your life and the lives of your family members. God bless you.

–Mary Ogenaarekhua

Acknowledgements

Thank You Lord for delivering me from evil and ungodly covenants that had hindered the generations before me and for making me a vessel that You now use to deliver others. You are GREAT and You are truly the BEST! There is none like You; I love You.

I thank **Apostles Alex and Rosetta Florence** of Joseph's Storehouse in Edmonton, Canada for their love and support. Thank you both for your desire to see people get set free from ungodly covenants. You have been a great encouragement to me and I love you both.

Lynne Garbinsky, there is none as persistent, devoted and motivating as you. Thanks a million for staying on me to finish this book and for the hours you spent helping me to transcribe and to edit the materials for this book. You are a great pal and I thank God for you.

Chapter 1

The Power of Covenants

I do sincerely believe that the things that I am about to discuss in this book are going to greatly impact your life if you get a hold of the spiritual principles that are involved. I am talking about covenants and understanding the power of covenants. If you do not understand covenants, you will not be able to go a long way with the Lord. The reason is because our God is a God of covenant. He keeps His covenants and He expects us to do the same. His name, **Jehovah** means the God who keeps covenants!

Covenant Defined:

The dictionary defines a **covenant as a binding agreement between two or more persons or parties. It is a formal sealed contract or agreement.** God uses covenants and His covenants are life giving. He said to us in **Jeremiah 29:11:**

> "For I know the plans I have for you, declares
> the Lord, <u>plans to prosper you and not to harm
> you</u>, plans to give you hope and a future."

Later, you will see as you read further that God does not operate outside of covenants. The devil uses covenants to operate in people's lives as well. His covenants are not life giving. Their end is death and destruction. He will try by all means to get you into an evil covenant with him and when you do, he is very legalistic and he will wave it in your life or in your children's lives forever. You can ignorantly make a covenant with the devil either with your words or your actions and he will use it against you all of your life. He functions only where there is ignorance, lack of knowledge and "zeal without knowledge" because there are a lot of people that try to operate biblical principles with a zeal but lack the knowledge of

God's Word and its application. Many people want to do things for God without asking God how He wants them done or if He even wants the things done and by so doing they open doors to the devil in their lives. When God sends you to do something, He equips you, provides for you and protects you.

How to Recognize an Evil Covenant:

When you look at your life and you see areas that you have been praying and you have been trying to get a breakthrough but nothing seems to be happening in that area, the next thing you need to do is go to the Lord and ask for clarification on your situation. He told me that if I pray and pray about a situation and I do not see a release, I need to stop and ask Him what caused the situation. He wants me to ask Him what the genesis (beginning) of the situation is; ask Him what is going on because in these types of situations, I might be dealing with a covenant that I or the generations before me made with the devil. When you are dealing with an evil covenant, nothing will change until that covenant is revealed and renounced because our God is a God that keeps covenants and the devil knows this very well. If you do not believe me, then look at anybody that is not yet born again; they are under the covenant that Adam made with the devil and it is still a valid covenant in their lives today!

I believe that it is critical for us to understand how we are making covenants in our lives so that we can operate God's kingdom principles effectively and so that we can keep from making covenants with the devil ignorantly. Ungodly covenants hinder us and they make our prayers ineffective because each time we pray, all the devil has to do is point to the active covenant that we have with him concerning the situation.

The Power of the Abrahamic Covenant in Our Lives Today:

Let us see the power of a covenant as outlined by God. It begins in **Genesis 15:5-6** when God came to visit Abram and He promised Abram a seed that will become a multitude even though Abram was old and childless. During one of His visits, God told Abram to look towards the heaven and the stars and that just as he cannot count the number of the stars in the sky, so shall he not be able to count the number of seed that He was going to give him. This was a great promise to a childless man that was a hundred years old and whose wife was ninety years old:

> **"And he brought him forth abroad, and said, <u>Look now toward heaven, and tell the stars, if thou be able to number them: and he said unto him, So shall thy seed be</u>. *6* And he believed in the LORD; and he counted it to him for righteousness."**

Although Abram believed God, he wanted an assurance about what God was telling him:

> "**And he** *(Abram)* **said, Lord GOD, <u>whereby shall I know that I shall inherit it</u>?**" (Genesis 15:8).

Upon hearing Abram's request for assurance, God decided to make a covenant with Abram and the covenant will seal the promise forever. Therefore, let us look at the very first covenant that God established with Abram because we are now partakers of this same covenant through the blood of Jesus. The Lord Jesus has by His own blood and by the New Testament made us (believers) the seed of Abraham. As a result, we can now partake of the ***Abrahamic Covenant.*** Also, be aware that this covenant is still very much in place in our lives today because if you are the seed of Abraham through His Son Jesus, God also made this covenant with you in Abraham. In reply to Abraham's question, God said to Abraham in **Genesis 15:9-21**:

> **"And he** *(God)* **said unto him, <u>Take me an heifer of three years old, and a she goat of three years old,</u> and <u>a ram of three years old,</u> and <u>a turtledove,</u> and <u>a young pigeon</u>.** (*See God is talking to Abram; He is telling him the things He needs in order to make a covenant with him.*) *10* **And he took unto him all**

these, and <u>divided them in the midst, and laid each piece one against another</u>: but the birds divided he not. *11* And when the fowls came down upon the carcases, Abram drove them away. *12* And when the sun was going down, a deep sleep fell upon Abram; and, lo, an horror of great darkness fell upon him. *13* And he said unto Abram, Know of a surety that thy seed shall be a stranger in a land that is not theirs, and shall serve them; and they shall afflict them four hundred years; *14* And also that nation, whom they shall serve, will I judge: and afterward shall they come out with great substance. *(God gives Abram a prophecy about his descendants.)* *15* And thou shalt go to thy fathers in peace; thou shalt be buried in a good old age. *16* But in the fourth generation they shall come hither again: for the iniquity of the Amorites is not yet full. *17* <u>And it came to pass, that,</u> <u>when the sun went down, and it was dark,</u> <u>behold a smoking furnace, and a burning lamp that passed between those pieces</u>. *(Now, this is the covenant—the Lord Himself passes through the pieces.)* *18* <u>In the same day the LORD made a covenant with Abram</u>, saying, Unto thy seed have I given this land, from the river of Egypt unto the great river, the river Euphrates: *19* The Kenites, and the Kenizzites, and the Kadmonites, *20* And the Hittites, and the Perizzites, and the Rephaims, *21* And the Amorites, and the Canaanites, and the Girgashites, and the Jebusites.

As you can see from these scriptures, Abraham laid the piece of the animals that he had divided one beside another and in the night time, a burning lamp (God) came and passed through the pieces. Killing and dividing the animals means that it is a permanent covenant and when God Himself came down, He passed through the midst of the dead animals. If you know anything about the eastern culture, you will notice that covenants are cut with lamps. Remember the story about the ten virgins, that were invited to the marriage covenant and five of them were wise and five of them were foolish? The five without oil were called foolish because their lamps had no oil so they could not turn their lights on to burn in order to cut a marriage covenant. As stated above, **God the Father came down as that burning furnace and passed through the pieces and what this means is that God willingly put Himself under the curse of death if He ever violates the covenant!**

God's blessing to Abraham and his seed is stated as follows:

"As for me, behold, my covenant is with thee, and thou shalt be a father of many nations. 5 Neither shall thy name any more be called Abram, but thy name shall be Abraham; for a father of many nations have I made thee. 6 <u>And I will make thee exceeding fruitful</u>, <u>and I will make nations of thee</u>, <u>and kings shall come out of thee</u>. 7 <u>And I will establish my covenant between me and thee and thy seed after thee in their generations for an everlasting covenant</u>, <u>to be a God unto thee, and to thy seed after thee</u>. 8 <u>And I will give unto thee, and to thy seed after thee, the land wherein thou art a stranger</u>, all the land of Canaan, for an everlasting possession; and I will be their God" (Genesis 17:4-8).

"<u>And I will make of thee a great nation</u>, and <u>I will bless thee</u>, and <u>make thy name great</u>; and <u>thou shalt be a blessing</u>: 3 And <u>I will bless them that bless thee</u>, and <u>curse him that curseth thee</u>: and <u>in thee shall all families of the earth be blessed</u>" (Genesis 12:2-3).

"That <u>in blessing I will bless thee</u>, and <u>in multiplying I will multiply thy seed</u> as the stars of the heaven, and as the sand which is upon the sea

shore; and <u>**thy seed shall possess the gate of his enemies;**</u> *18* And <u>**in thy seed shall all the nations of the earth be blessed**</u>; because thou hast obeyed my voice" (Genesis 22:17-18).

As you can see from the above scriptures any man or woman on planet earth that wants to be truly blessed needs to partake of the Abrahamic Covenant. There is no other way out because God has put every man's blessing in Abraham —**"in thee shall all the families of the earth be blessed."** The Lord Jesus made the believers (us) partakers of the Abrahamic Covenant by making us the seed of Abraham in Himself. This is the covenant that we have with God today through His Son.

The Consequences of Violating the Abrahamic Covenant:

According to this covenant between God, Abraham and Abraham's seed, the fate of whosoever among them that violates the covenant will be like the fate of the dead animals! This is why the scripture says that the **"soul that sinneth, it shall die"** in **Ezekiel 18:4.** What God was saying to Abraham and Abraham's seed is very profound and powerful because according to the terms of this covenant whoever will violates this covenant that I just made with you Abraham; either you, your seed or I, will end up like these dead animals.

If you transgress the Abrahamic Covenant, death is the result. When you transgress God's covenant, you bring on yourself the curse and the fate of those dead animals. **This is applicable to whoever violates the covenant and it is one of the reasons why God can never violate the covenant that He made with Abraham and Abraham's seed. He willingly placed Himself under the curse of death if He does.**

As you can see from God's perspective, covenants are very powerful and very serious. They are not to be taken lightly. We are to know what they involve and how they impact our lives. For example, according to the Bible, **"Whoso findeth a wife findeth a good thing, <u>and obtaineth favour of the LORD</u>."** We know that marriage is the most serious covenant concerning the family. If according to God's kingdom principle (covenant) finding a wife gives a man favor before God, what happens then to the man when he abandons his wife and family for another woman? What happens to the man or woman who negates his or her marriage covenant because of another man or woman?

We find the answer to this in **Malachi 2:13-14:**

"<u>And this have ye done again, covering the altar of the LORD with tears, with weeping,</u> and <u>with crying out, insomuch that he regardeth not the offering</u> *(prayer)* **<u>any more, or receiveth it with good will at your hand.</u> 14 Yet ye say, <u>Wherefore</u>? <u>Because the LORD hath been witness between thee and the wife of thy youth, against whom thou hast dealt treacherously: yet is she thy companion, and the wife of thy covenant.</u>"**

As you can see from the Lord's perspective, when a man mistreats his wife or abandons her for another woman, **God Himself becomes a witness against the man and He will no longer receive the man's prayers, offerings or praise!** The man might think that because he married his mistress after divorcing his wife that he is OK with God but the truth of the matter is, according to God's covenant principle, that man has an indictment against him in heaven and is no longer in favor with God. Therefore, we all must understand the power of covenants.

Before you take it upon yourself to make verbal promises and covenant with the Lord, make sure that you will fulfill your covenant promise. Some men in the Old Testament that took it upon themselves to make a covenant with the Lord on their own initiative and God judged them for not keeping the covenant. This is recorded in **Jeremiah 34:15-18:**

> "...<u>ye had made a covenant before me in the house which is called by my name</u>... *17* Therefore thus saith the LORD; Ye have not hearkened unto me... <u>behold, I proclaim a liberty for you, saith the LORD, to the sword, to the pestilence,</u> and <u>to the famine</u>; and <u>I will make you to be removed into all the kingdoms of the earth</u>. *18* And **<u>I will give the men that have transgressed my covenant, which have not performed the words of the covenant</u>** which they had made before me, when they cut the calf in twain, and passed between the parts thereof."

Therefore, it is better not to promise God something if you know that you are not going to do it because God judges covenant breakers.

God's Covenant with the Children of Israel:

As I stated before, God operates in His dealings with man through covenants. When He brought the children of Israel out of Egypt, He gave them a covenant of conduct called the LAW. We know it as the Ten Commandments. God promised everyone in this covenant a lot of blessings if they obey the terms of the covenant. We see this is **Deuteronomy 28:1-14:**

> "And it shall come to pass, if thou shalt hearken diligently unto the voice of the LORD thy God, to observe and to do all his commandments which I command thee this day, that the LORD thy God will set thee on high above all nations of the earth: *2* <u>And all these blessings shall come on thee, and overtake thee, if thou shalt hearken unto the voice of the LORD thy God</u>. *3* <u>Blessed shalt thou be in the city,</u> and <u>blessed shalt thou be in the field</u>. *4* <u>Blessed shall be the fruit of thy</u>

body, and the fruit of thy ground, and the fruit of thy cattle, the increase of thy kine, and the flocks of thy sheep. *5* Blessed shall be thy basket and thy store. *6* Blessed shalt thou be when thou comest in, and blessed shalt thou be when thou goest out. *7* The LORD shall cause thine enemies that rise up against thee to be smitten before thy face: they shall come out against thee one way, and flee before thee seven ways. *8* The LORD shall command the blessing upon thee in thy storehouses, and in all that thou settest thine hand unto; and he shall bless thee in the land which the LORD thy God giveth thee. *9* The LORD shall establish thee an holy people unto himself, as he hath sworn unto thee, if thou shalt keep the commandments of the LORD thy God, and walk in his ways. *10* And all people of the earth shall see that thou art called by the name of the LORD; and they shall be afraid of thee. *11* And the LORD shall make thee plenteous in goods, in the fruit of thy body, and in the fruit of thy cattle, and in the fruit of thy ground, in the land which the LORD sware unto thy fathers to give thee. *12* The LORD shall open unto thee his good treasure, the heaven to give the rain unto thy land in his season, and to bless all the work of thine hand: and thou shalt lend unto many nations, and thou shalt not borrow. *13* And the LORD shall make thee the head, and not the tail; and thou shalt be above only, and thou shalt not be beneath; if that thou hearken unto the commandments of the LORD thy God, which I command thee this day, to observe and to do them: *14* And thou shalt not go aside from any of the words which I command thee this day, to the right hand, or to the left, to go after other gods to serve them."

We know according to the same chapter that those who violate the terms of this covenant have a great deal of curses heap upon them according to **Deuteronomy 28:15-32** below:

> "But it shall come to pass, if thou wilt not hearken unto the voice of the LORD thy God, to observe to do all his commandments and his statutes which I command thee this day; that all these curses shall come upon thee, and overtake thee: *16* <u>Cursed shalt thou be in the city</u>, and <u>cursed shalt thou be in the field</u>. *17* <u>Cursed shall be thy basket and thy store</u>. *18* <u>Cursed shall be the fruit of thy body</u>, and <u>the fruit of thy land</u>, the increase of thy kine, and the flocks of thy sheep. *19* <u>Cursed shalt thou be when thou comest in</u>, and <u>cursed shalt thou be when thou goest out</u>. *20* <u>The LORD shall send upon thee cursing, vexation, and rebuke, in all that thou settest thine hand unto for to do, until thou be destroyed, and until thou perish quickly</u>; because of the wickedness of thy doings, whereby thou hast forsaken me… The LORD shall cause thee to be smitten before thine enemies: thou shalt go out one way against them, and flee seven ways before them: and shalt be removed into all the kingdoms of the earth. *26* And thy carcase shall be meat unto all fowls of the air, and unto the beasts of the earth, and no man shall fray them away. *27* The LORD will smite thee with the botch of Egypt, and with the emerods, and with the scab, and with the itch, whereof thou canst not be healed. *28* The LORD shall smite thee with madness, and blindness, and astonishment of heart: *29* And thou shalt grope at noonday, as the blind gropeth in darkness, and thou shalt not prosper in thy ways: and thou shalt be only oppressed and spoiled evermore, and no man shall save thee. *30* Thou shalt betroth a wife, and another man shall lie with her: thou shalt build

an house, and thou shalt not dwell therein: thou shalt plant a vineyard, and shalt not gather the grapes thereof. *31* **Thine ox shall be slain before thine eyes, and thou shalt not eat thereof: thine ass shall be violently taken away from before thy face, and shall not be restored to thee: thy sheep shall be given unto thine enemies, and thou shalt have none to rescue them."**

I did not list all of the curses in Deuteronomy Chapter 28 in the above list of curses because they are too many. You need to read them for yourself. These curses should make anyone not want to violate the terms of the covenant. As we are aware, the children of Israel constantly violated the terms of this covenant and each time God punished them as He promised. Finally, He promised them a new covenant in which He will write the laws in their hearts and not on tables of stones anymore. We see this in **Jeremiah 31:31**, **Hebrews 8:10**, and **Hebrews 10: 16**.

> "<u>The time is coming, declares the Lord, when I will make a new covenant with the house of Israel and with the house of Judah</u>" (Jeremiah 31:31).

It is restated in **Hebrews 8:10** below:

> "<u>For this is the covenant that I will make with the house of Israel after those days</u>, saith the Lord; <u>I will put my laws into their mind, and write them in their hearts</u>: and <u>I will be to them a God, and they shall be to me a people</u>."

In **Hebrews 10:16** it says:

> "<u>This is the covenant that I will make with them after those days, saith the Lord, I will put my laws into their hearts, and in their minds will I write them</u>."

This is where the Lord Jesus comes in. God the Father fulfilled His promise to make a new covenant with the children of Israel by sending His Son, Jesus Christ. The Lord established this New Covenant in His blood. This New Covenant is designed by God to open the door for those who believe in what He did through His Son (provided salvation) to receive the benefits of the **Abrahamic Covenant**. God's covenant promise to Abraham is that through Abraham shall all the families of the earth be blessed and God fulfilled this promise in His Son, Jesus Christ. Today, anyone in the world who believes the finished works of Jesus Christ (the seed of Abraham) will become a partaker of the blessings of Abraham through Him!

The Everlasting Covenant that the Lord Jesus Established:

The following scripture shows us how the Lord Jesus brought us into a covenant relationship (into the Abrahamic Covenant) with His Father by His shed blood. This covenant is an Everlasting Covenant. We see it as reported in **Matthew 26:26-28:**

> **"And as they were eating, Jesus took bread, and blessed it, and brake it, and gave it to the disciples, and said, <u>Take, eat; this is my body</u>. *27* And <u>he took the cup</u>, and <u>gave thanks</u>, and <u>gave it to them, saying, Drink ye all of it</u>; *28* <u>For this is my blood of the new testament</u>** *(covenant)*, **<u>which is shed for many for the remission of sins</u>."**

> **"For I have received of the Lord that which also I delivered unto you, That the Lord Jesus the same night in which he was betrayed took bread:** *24* **And when he had given thanks, <u>he brake it, and said, Take, eat: this is my body, which is broken for you: this do in remembrance of me</u>. After the same manner also <u>he took the cup, when he had supped, saying, This cup is the new testament</u>**

in my blood: this do ye, as oft as ye drink it, in remembrance of me" (1 Corinthians 11:23-24).

The Lord Jesus paid with His own blood to bring us into the New Covenant. God had to annul the covenant (law) that He made with the children of Israel in the wilderness because they constantly disobeyed the covenant. Today, God has given us a new covenant in Christ and in this New Covenant, the laws are written in our hearts but we must always remember that the covenant that God made with Abraham was in place before ever He gave the LAW to the children of Israel. That Abrahamic Covenant as I said before is an Everlasting Covenant and it is still in effect in our lives today. We became partakers of the Abrahamic blessings by virtue of the covenant that we have with the Lord Jesus. Both covenants are blood covenants. They both speak life or death; life to those who obey and death to those who do not obey. The Lord said in Mark 16:16 that, **"He that believeth and is baptized shall be saved; but he that believeth not shall be damned."**

According to God's plan, you have to be born again to become His new creation, become a partaker of the new covenant that Jesus established with His blood and then God can begin to exercise His legal rights to work on your behalf according to the terms of the covenant with Abraham. You will then have legal rights to use the name of the Lord Jesus and you will have access to the covenant blessings in Abraham. You have to remember the significance of the animals in the Covenant between God and Abraham that were cut into pieces. Meaning that as a partaker of this covenant, you have to understand the terms of it because God put Himself and whosoever violates the covenant under the curse of death. This is serious and all believers must remind themselves of the fact that whenever they transgress the covenant of the Lord, they are essentially pronouncing that death sentence on themselves because God made the covenant with Abraham and his seed after him forever. We are grafted into the Jewish race (Israel) by the blood of Jesus but this does not mean that God has done away with the children of Israel because He has not. The majority of them missed the first opportunity that the Lord gave them to partake of the New Covenant but He is going to give them another opportunity to be saved. God loves Israel and He never gives up on her.

When you look at the life of Jesus, you can also see the power of covenant in operation. For instance, whenever the Jewish leaders and their supporters did not like what the Lord preached, they would try to either stone Him or throw Him down the cliff. Their intentions were always to stop Him by killing Him but they could not. The Bible always reports that He just passed through their midst and went on His way. One day the Lord showed me how He immediately became vulnerable the minute He cut the New Testament Covenant with the disciples. For the very first time in His existence, the devil now had a way to get to Him through Judas Iscariot. By the virtue of the New Covenant, the Lord became a brother to the disciples including Judas and Judas became the open door for the devil to get to the Lord.

Judas Betrayal of a Covenant Brother:

It matters who you come into a covenant relationship with. It can bring you blessings or curses depending on whose servant they are. The Lord knew what was going to happen but He said woe to the man through whom it will happen. It is the reason why Judas is called the son of perdition. He was a covenant breaker; he betrayed one who had become his own brother!

This is why when you hear about the betrayal of Judas and you compare it with Peter's sin of rejecting Jesus, you might wonder which is greater or a more serious sin but when you begin to understand what it means for you to brake a covenant, you will see that Judas's sin is the more serious one. It was a great betrayal for someone to sell out a covenant brother and it is a very serious sin in God's book. Covenants are important to God and they are very useful and valuable in His kingdom. We are Christians today because we have a covenant with God the Father by the blood of His

Son, Jesus Christ. If you choose today to no longer be a partaker of the covenant, you can walk away freely. God will never reject you but you can of your own free will walk away from Him and from His covenant.

When we came into the Kingdom of God, something happened to us that brought us into this powerful relationship with God and we need to begin to understand how God operates His kingdom through His covenant principles. When you begin to understand how God operates through the power of covenant, you also get a glimpse of how the devil tries to come into your life because whatever God does, the devil tries to counterfeit. Let us look at **Romans 8:15** which tells us how this New Covenant in the blood of Jesus now covers us.

> **"For ye have not received the spirit of bondage again to fear; but <u>ye have received the Spirit of adoption, whereby we cry, Abba, Father</u>."**

Again, I say that we were grafted into the **Abrahamic Covenant** by the blood of Jesus. God accomplished this through the process of adoption. It means that we have been grafted into the "True Vine" (Israel) and that we have become the seed of Abraham because as I said before, when God made the covenant with Abraham, He also made it with Abraham's seed forever. The above scripture tells us that God has adopted us as His children and that we have not received the spirit of bondage but the spirit of adoption whereby we Gentiles can cry, "Abba, Father" and He will respond to us according to the terms of His covenant with Abraham and his seed. So, you can see that we are in a very powerful covenant with God the Father, God the Son and God the Holy Spirit.

Covenant Benefits and Position in the Kingdom of God:

If you read **Romans 8:17**, you will notice that it tells us that we are not just God's children but that we have become heirs of God and joint heirs with Christ:

> "And if children, <u>then heirs</u>; <u>heirs of God, and joint-heirs with Christ</u>; if so be that we suffer with him, that we may be also glorified together."

God the Father has made His Son Jesus, the Lord over all of His creation and the Lord reigns from heaven over all. As joint heirs with Him, it means that we are also reigning on earth as the extension (the body of Christ) of our Lord who is the head of His church. Remember when God told Abraham in **Genesis 13:14** to look **"northward, and southward, and eastward, and westward"** and Abraham extended his vision far into the heavens and according to **Genesis 14:19**, Abraham by faith became **"the possessor of heaven and earth."** If you want to see the power of the extension of Abraham's faith and its manifestation, take a look at the Lord Jesus who is the seed of Abraham to whom all the promises pertain. This is recorded in **Galatians 3:16**:

> "<u>Now to Abraham and his seed were the promises made</u>. He saith not, And to seeds, as of many; but as of one, <u>And to thy seed, which is Christ</u>."

To prove this, you will see that today and forever, the Lord Jesus sits on the Right Hand of God the Father and rules the earth from heaven using His church. We, who are also the seed of Abraham in Christ and the children of the Living God through a covenant, are co-reigning with Christ with His delegated authority.

We just found out in **Romans 8:17** that we are joint heirs with Christ but **Galatians 4:1** says that of you do not know your rights and if you do not really know who you are, you are not different from a servant:

"Now I say, **That the heir, as long as he is a child, differeth nothing from a servant, though he be lord of all**;"

God has given us great and precious things in Christ but until we know these things and apprehend them for ourselves, we loose out on their benefits. We are called to be heirs of God and joints heirs with Christ but very many of us live like paupers. The reason is because many do not know what they have been given and those that do know are not correctly applying the principles of God that will enable them to appropriate what has been given to them. This is why **Ecclesiastes 10:7** says:

"**I have seen servants upon horses**, and **princes walking as servants** upon the earth."

This is an inverted pyramid because many of the believers who are ordained and given all the blessings are the ones struggling while the heathens are living it up or having it good. We are the salt of the earth, we are the ones that God has placed on earth to have dominion but when you look at a lot of Christians, you will see that many are looking for jobs, have no place to stay, do not have a car and no money. Then, you have the ones whose spouses have just simply walked away and are left to care for all the children alone.

As I see these things, I begin to wonder and say to myself, "Why in the world are we going through all these things as Christians?" One day the Lord said to me, "The reason that you see all these things in my house is because you guys do not understand the power of covenants." According to Him, if we understand His nature as God, we will realize that it is His nature to cut covenants. He created this earth but He willingly gave the earth to the children of men. He then set it up to operate in partnership with man by making covenant with man. After the flood, the first thing He did was to cut a covenant with Noah, the earth and every living thing. We read this in **Genesis 9:12-15**:

"**And God said, <u>This is the token of the covenant which I make between me and you and every living creature that is with you, for perpetual generations</u>:** *13 I do set my bow in the cloud, and it shall be for a token of a covenant between me and the earth. 14* <u>**And it shall come to pass, when I bring a cloud over the earth, that the bow shall be seen in the cloud:**</u> *15* <u>**And I will remember my covenant, which is between me and you and every living creature of all flesh;**</u> **and <u>the waters shall no more become a flood to destroy all flesh</u>.**"

God remembers His covenants and He wants us to remember them also. Because He has willingly given man dominion over the earth, He always consults with a man or a woman on earth before He does anything on earth. When He wants to operate or do something on earth, He looks for somebody; a human being that is on His side that will help give a voice in the earth realm to what He is planning to do. This is a very powerful kingdom principle with God and it is the reason why those who wait for God to do everything for them while they do nothing, live a life of defeat.

The devil always tries to counterfeit what our God does. Therefore, you see the kingdom of darkness (the devil) trying to mimic or do a similar thing in order to accomplish his evil desires. He too will look for someone who will help give a voice to his evil plans so that they can also come to pass. **God created us and He put in our tongue, the power to speak life and the power to speak death.** Always remember that God set out to make man in His image and after His likeness. **In other words, a man who can make a decree, a man who can command the elements, a man who can change circumstances and a man who can look and say, "this is ungodly and it needs to go."** It was a big chance that God took when He decided to create man and it has cost Him a lot because of what we have put Him through. He counted the cost in the beginning and was willing to pay the price to reap a godly seed in Christ at the end.

When all is accomplished according to God's plan, He is going to have all these children in all of eternity that are not only in His image but have His character. They will love righteousness and even when no one is watching, they are going to say no to evil and always yes to righteousness. They will exercise His power and as they speak, things will happen to cause change.

God Wants a Being that He Can Relate To:

This is what He wanted; a being of His own class that He can relate to. That is why when you see the new man in the realm of the spirit being crowned or being ordained by God, you will think that you are looking at Jesus but when you look closer, you then discover that it is a born again Christian that has put on Christ. We the new creation have put on Christ and as a result, we look like Him even though we still retain our individual identities.

> **"For as many of you as have been <u>baptized into Christ have put on Christ</u>"** (Galatians 3:27).

All heaven respects the new creation and honors her. She enjoys the privileges that an heir of God is entitled to because she is one with the Head —the Lord Jesus! This is why angels are in awe about this new creation because we are clothed with the very Son of God.

From all these, you can see that because we are in a relationship with God through a covenant, we have a very unique place in His kingdom and in His creation. You also have to remember that by the power of the same covenant, we are now partakers of His divine nature. For those that may not be aware of who we have become in Christ Jesus, I am referring to **2 Peter 1:4**:

> **"Whereby are given unto us exceeding great and precious promises: <u>that by these ye might be partakers of the divine nature</u>, having escaped the corruption that is in the world through lust."**

Because of this same covenant, we are not to partake of the evil that is now prevalent in the world. We have power in the name of Jesus and we have the delegated authority that the Lord gave us in His name. We are to reign over sicknesses, diseases, wickedness, the devil and all his evil spirits. We are to use the name of Jesus to exercise dominion, to subdue and to replenish the earth because we are in a covenant with God through the blood of His Son. Jesus said to us in **Mark 16:17-18**:

> "And <u>these signs shall follow them that believe; In my name shall they cast out devils; they shall speak with new tongues; They shall take up serpents; and if they drink any deadly thing, it shall not hurt them; they shall lay hands on the sick, and they shall recover.</u>"

The reason we can do all these things is again because of a covenant. This covenant that Jesus established with His blood guarantees and empowers us to go against rebellious spirits and to pull them down. We are no longer ordinary people. We are now what the Bible calls a very unique people according to **1 Peter 2:9**:

> "But <u>ye are a chosen generation</u>, <u>a royal priesthood</u>, <u>an holy nation</u>, a <u>peculiar people</u>; that ye should shew forth the praises of him who hath called you out of darkness into his marvellous light:"

We the believers are the only ones that have been given this power and authority. If you do not believe it, take a look at **Acts 19:14-15** and read about the seven Sons of Sceva who went up to a man possessed with an evil spirit and tried to cast out the evil spirit without being in a covenant relationship with the Lord. The evil spirit jumped on them, beat them up and drove them away naked and wounded.

> "**Then certain of the vagabond Jews, exorcists, took upon them to call over them which had evil**

spirits the name of the Lord Jesus, saying, <u>We adjure you by Jesus whom Paul preacheth</u>. *14* And there were seven sons of one Sceva, a Jew, and chief of the priests, which did so. *15* <u>And the evil spirit answered and said, Jesus I know, and Paul I know; but who are ye</u>? *16* And the man in whom the evil spirit was leaped on them, and overcame them, and prevailed against them, so that they fled out of that house naked and wounded. And there were seven sons of one Sceva, a Jew, and chief of the priests, which did so. And the evil spirit answered and said, Jesus I know, and Paul I know; but who are ye?

What the evil spirit was saying to them was, "I do not see the mark of the covenant on you. You are not covered by the blood of Jesus and as a result, you have no authority to cast me out." They were not partakers of the Everlasting Covenant and as a result have no right to its benefits of which casting out devils is one.

All Believers Have the Mark of Jesus on Their Foreheads:

The Lord puts His mark on all who believe in Him and we are covered by His blood. I was amazed to see me as a new creation in the realm of the Spirit. I used to wonder why people would rise up against me before they even got to know me in some of the places that I went to or in the workplace until I saw the new creation that I have become in Christ Jesus. For those of you who have bosses that rise up against you in the workplace and people who rise up against you for no apparent reason, there is a reason. You know what I am talking about; you walk through the door and you have not done anything and the people do not know you but they are already out against you. It seems as if there was an email sent out to tell them that you were coming and that they should be armed against you. I used to wonder why these things happen until the Lord opened my eyes to see what we the believers have on our foreheads —the name **JESUS** written in His bright red blood! When I saw how we the believers look in the realm of the spirit, I was like, "Oh my God, the name JESUS is written on our foreheads in His blood! He said, "Now, you know why you don't have to do anything to provoke anybody in the places that you go." This is why the Bible says that we are sealed with the blood of Jesus.

Therefore, when we the believers walk into a place, the blood of Jesus on our foreheads makes the evil spirits in the place to become very uncomfortable. The spirits will not want you around and as a result, they provoke the people in the place to try and get rid of you. You do not have to do anything to make the ungodly people rise up against you because the evil spirits in them are agitated by the power of the blood of Jesus that is upon you. Everything that is ungodly in that place will not want you around. If you have been in this type of situation at your home or in your workplace, I hope that this information will help you to understand why certain ones cannot stand you or are out against you for no reason. Be encouraged because the blood of Jesus will always protect you as a result of you being in an awesome covenant with the Living God.

Many believers have ungodly relatives that try to make their lives a living hell at home because they too are agitated by the blood of Jesus. A lot of Christians go to church, worship and praise the Lord but they go home to find some demon laden relatives just waiting to say or do something ugly to them. Some of those relatives might say things to you that can challenge even your salvation as you try to hold your peace. If you are one of such people, also be encouraged in what God has done in your life. He has sealed you with the blood of Jesus and you are His child by covenant. Also, if you have been wondering why they say and do those ugly things to you, now you know that it is because they are still under the covenant that Adam made with the devil but we the believers are operating based on the covenant that the Lord Jesus established with His blood. When Adam sinned, he willingly submitted himself and all his seed after him to the devil.

Yes, God always sets His mark on His children. He used the mark of circumcision with Abraham and a mark on the foreheads of those who cry out for righteousness in the days of Ezekiel. You can read this in the book of the Prophet Ezekiel in **Ezekiel 9:4.** Remember that an angel was sent to mark the foreheads of all those that cry out for righteousness?

> "**And the LORD said unto him, Go through the midst of the city, through the midst of Jerusalem, and <u>set a mark upon the foreheads of the men that sigh and that cry for all the abominations that be done in the midst thereof</u>.**"

The Lord Jesus also promised in **Revelation 3:12** to write His name upon those who overcome:

> "**Him that overcometh will I make a pillar in the temple of my God, and he shall go no more out: and I will write upon him the name of my God, and the name of the city of my God, which is new Jerusalem, which cometh down out of heaven from my God: <u>and I will write upon him my new name</u>.**"

We the believers overcome by the blood of Jesus and we are forever sealed by His blood. What I want you to understand from this is that we are these awesome beings in Christ. We are partakers of this awesome covenant with God and He has given us this awesome ability to be able to have fellowship with Him. He has given us the authority to go forth and to do wonderful and mighty things in the name of Jesus. Again, I say that every person alive today who is not yet born again is still under the Adamic Covenant and they have to, of their own free will, choose to come out of this covenant and become partakers of the covenant that the Lord Jesus established with His blood. This is why salvation is by choice; you have to freely renounce that Old Covenant with the devil and choose the New Covenant that Jesus established. If you refuse, then you do not have the right to go against the devil because you are still under his jurisdiction and therefore do not have the authority to cast him out. You cannot effectively use the name of Jesus because if you use the name of Jesus without the proper backup by the Holy Spirit, those evil spirits will come against you and mess your life up.

Making an Evil Covenant:

If you have an evil covenant with the devil whether you know it or not, he will always be able to defeat you or get one over you. He does not excuse you for your ignorance but rather rejoices because you do not know how he operates against you. What has happened to many of us in the past is that, the enemy has been able to come in and get us into ungodly covenants, vows, agreements and oaths and we walked away from them thinking that just because we left the place or the person, we are no longer bound by them. We truly believe that when we walk away from people, places and things that it is the end of the matter but the real truth of the matter is that walking away does not remove the promises, agreements, vows and oaths that we made whether they be oral or written, casual or formal. What happens is that the enemy actually begins a process of trying to enforce these things in our lives even though we had walked away from them. He knows that we have no understanding of our agreement with him and that ignorance allows him to operate unchallenged in our lives. As a matter of fact, he will go before God the Father to contend for his right to afflict us in those areas. He actually demands that God the Father deliver a person up to him in the area that he has a covenant with the person. It could even be that the person was not the one that made the covenant with him but the person's father or grandfather but because a covenant is a long standing agreement, he will try to enforce his right to the person in the area of the person's life that the covenant was made.

Examples of Evil Covenants in My Life:

A good example of an ungodly covenant in my life happened before I came to the United States and my mother at the time was not yet born again. Her brother took her to a female witchdoctor who was very much into spiritism. This means that the woman claims to communicate with the dead and with water spirits and she also claimed to spend seven to fourteen months at a time under water in the river with water spirits. According to her, this is how she gets her supernatural powers and instructions from the water spirits on what she is to do for people. These types of people are very common in Nigeria and many of them even operate churches. Just to tell you how the devil operates through people, mine was a case of being in the wrong place at the wrong time and I narrated it in pages 44-47 of my book titled, ***Unveiling the God-Mother*** in which I talked about the works of water spirits (the God-mother spirits). Below is an excerpt of how my mother and I made an evil covenant that I later paid for with many afflictions until the Lord showed me how to remove it from my life.

Excerpt:

Before I left my mother's hometown in my last months of high school, my mother came to visit during one of the school breaks. She had been referred to a female witchdoctor in a town close to her hometown. She was looking for a solution to one of my younger sisters' stubbornness. Since I was not the focus of this particular visit to the witchdoctor, I decided to go along with them in order to enjoy the car ride. I regretted my going on this trip for years afterwards. While my mother and my uncle went inside with my sister to consult with the witchdoctor, I stayed in the car with the driver and listened to music. Not long after they went in, they came out. The report was that this woman who claimed to have just returned from living under water for seven months with water spirits said that my sister and the rest of my mother's children were not the ones that my mother should focus on. She picked me out of all my mother's children as the one that my mother needed to be concerned about.

The non-Christian Ibos and non-Christian Delta (formerly Bendel) Ibos in Midwestern Nigeria believe in reincarnation. My mother is a Delta Ibo from Agbor. They believe that in the children's world before birth, there are a group of children (Ogbanje) that love coming into the world to gain the affections of their parents and relatives. Just when everyone is so in love with them, they exit the world only to return again. According to this belief, these children actually love to torment their parents by dying and returning again to the world only to die again. Therefore, it was the duty of the parents to identify such children and to stop them on their endless journey between life and death. According to this female witchdoctor that had not even laid eyes on me yet, I was to be apprehended before graduation from high school. I promptly told my mother and her brother that the woman was wrong and that I was not an Ogbanje. They both challenged me to go and stand before the woman in order to settle the issue. All she did when I went inside to see her was reaffirm her words. I was so angry with myself for accompanying my mother on this journey. My immediate younger sister did not come along on this journey; she was not around to be picked on.

My mother truly believed the woman's report that something evil was going to happen to me before or upon my graduation from high school if something was not done. She went about sad for two days because I would not listen to the witchdoctor's report. My mother, my grandmother, and my younger sister began to speak to me about the need to let the woman perform the ceremony to break the cycle of an endless journey in and out of life. We went back to the woman to inquire from her what needed to be done. She gave my mother a list of the things she needed to bring, **but before she could perform the ceremony,**

my mother had to obtain my genuine consent*. The ceremony cannot be performed against a person's will. She told my mother to give me whatever I asked for as a bargain for my willingness to undergo the ceremony. When she informed me, my sister and I thought about the possible things I could ask for. At first I chose a car but we decided against it because we knew she could not afford it. I settled for a party with my friends and a shopping spree.*

Because the Ogbanje ceremony is popular among the Ibos, somehow the news got to my dad in the city where he was. He found out the date of the Ogbanje ceremony and he promptly showed up in my mother's hometown. Since we were no longer children, my sister and I decided to verify whether or not the Ibos' claim of removing an Ogbanje spirit from a person was true. I think in his own way, my dad wanted also to find out the truth about the claim. On the appointed day, we all went to the town to meet with this woman for the ceremony. She claimed that there was a woman spirit (a "mermaid") living in the river near her home and that this mermaid was the one that gave her power. Therefore, the ceremony would take place in the river.

Again, yours truly was dressed in a white cloth with a pot full of concoctions placed on my head as I was led in a procession to this river. It was the most shameful experience of my life. According to her, the spirit was in the head and had to be removed. I was made to lie down in the shallow part of the river while she made an incision on the left side of my face. Since the incision was close to my left eye, I was determined to see what the spirit looked like. I mean, I was not going to miss a thing. I watched as she in a very subtle way pulled out something that looked like a piece of gold wrapped with a black thread from the sand next to my head and began to show it to the people that stood by as the Ogbanje spirit that she pulled out of my head. I immediately told my mother, my sister, and my dad that it was not true and that I saw her take the piece of gold from the sand next to my head. She replied that I was making such statements because of my desire not to be rid of the spirit. But I knew what I saw. She conducted a funeral for the piece of gold.

When I obtained a visa to come to the United States, again my mother went for another consultation and was told this time that she needed to do something else so that I did not come back from the United States in a casket. This time she had the ace. No ceremony, no U.S. for me! The woman who conducted this second ceremony could not circumcise me because I was already grown so she made an incision on my stomach. There was no procession in this ceremony.

Before the above events, I had also been dedicated by my grandmother and declared to be the "godmother" to the god that my family was serving before they became Muslims. Everyone in my family was to reverence my head as a respect to the god. As I grew up and enrolled in school, I discovered that it was not socially comfortable to answer the name of a god or to be a "godmother" and I rejected the name. The other children did not like the idea of playing with some mother of a god because it made them afraid. I also renounced Islam and all the Muslim activities and I eventually became born again. Although I had walked away from these things, I did not address the covenants that they represented with the devil. Therefore, the devil was still holding them as valid covenant agreements against me. He was furiously trying to enforce these covenants and the resulting consequence was that I constantly had to deal with serious life threatening situations in my life.

One day, I was lying down and I saw in a vision the devil standing before the Lord contending for my head. He was demanding that the Lord deliver up my head to him because according to him, it belongs to him and that it was given to him by the dedication that the witchdoctor made with my head. Also, I saw him pointing to the mark beside my left eye that the witchdoctor had made on my face as a proof of the right that he had to my head! What the Lord did in His mercy was to open heaven so that I could see what was going on in the spiritual realm concerning my head. When I saw the devil's contention for my head, I knew exactly what he was getting at and I knew that he was using my past dedication ceremonies as a legal right to own my head. I also knew that I was of age when I took part in the last two dedication ceremonies so I had sinned against God and it had given the devil an open door against me.

When I got up from that state of the vision, I went to the Lord and I repented for the dedication and for the ceremonies. I renounced the procession and everything idolatrous that my family and I had been involved in. I asked the Lord to take the white cloth that I was clothed with away and to destroy the pot that was placed on my head. I renounced everything that we did at the river and I declared that I was no longer in the river with the witchdoctor. I repented of all the covenants and agreements that they had represented with the devil and I asked the Lord the wipe away the mark beside my left eye with the blood of Jesus. I then dedicated my life, my head and everything about me to the Lord. Since then, I have not seen the devil contending for my head again. Afterwards, the Lord showed me that most of my afflictions have been over my head because of the evil covenants. I suffered a fatal fall with my head, suffered mental afflictions and several near miss accidents!

It was then that I remembered that when I was dedicated as a godmother, there was a pronouncement that everyone in my father's family was to reverence my head. The belief was that anyone who touches my head irreverently would be plagued because it was a great disrespect to the idol god for anyone to touch his mother's head without reverence. I realized that I needed to go back and undo those evil covenants that were made on my behalf because when I took that fatal fall, it was my head that hit the metal banister and it was what killed me. Prior to the Lord's revelation to me through that vision, I had no idea that there had always been a contention over my head because of the evil dedication ceremonies and verbal pronouncements over my head by my grandmother. I was free after I repented and renounced the agreements that they represented with the devil.

You never know how past evil covenants impact your daily life until the Lord reveals them to you. Yours might not be as drastic as mine because you may not have come out of a family that was steeped into idolatry the way mine was, but still, negative or ungodly covenants that you and members of your family made on your behalf will impact your life more than you can know or imagine. They can keep you from getting a decent job, from being successfully married or married at all, and they can keep you in sicknesses and diseases.

The Power and Effect of the Ungodly Words of a Parent:

Another ungodly covenant that my mother made on my behalf had to do with employment. Just like any other mother, she was proud of me when I finished high school at the top of my class. She was working in a fabric manufacturing company and she wanted the joy of having her daughter work in the personnel office of her company. It was a big deal for one of the employees to have his or her child work in the personnel office. Therefore, she spoke with her manager about me working as his secretary (Administrative Assistant). The problem was that I did not want to be a secretary and I did not want to work in the company where she works.

From the time that I was little and in the village, I would look up at a plane flying high in the sky and say, "One day, I am going to get in a plane and go to wherever they go." Although I had no idea where they were flying, I knew that one day, I was going to get in one and fly to where ever they went. I also knew that one day,

I would have my own secretary so I refused to settle for anything less. Therefore, when her boss called me in for an interview, I told him that I was not interested in working for him. I told him not to let my mother know but to just inform her that I did not do well in the interview. That was how I got myself out of that situation and I thought it was all behind me forever.

To God's glory, I came to the United States and I received a Bachelor and a Masters degree and I immediately got a job with the New York State Department of Labor. I was groomed for two years by the Rockefeller Institute of Management for higher level management positions with the New York State government. In those two years, I was attached to department directors and their top commissioners for on the job training. After three years of working at the Department of Labor, I got saved during one of my visits to Nigeria and my priorities changed when God the Father walked into my bedroom and He spoke to me for six hours. It was an awesome visitation and He blessed me.

After He left, another entity (the devil) also showed up and began to talk and to taunt me. I ended up in the psychiatric hospital not even up to a week after God the Father's visit. I was in shock because His visit is the biggest thing that can happen to a person but for me, it opened up the spiritual part of my life that I did not know how to deal with. I knew nothing about the Bible besides a few verses in Matthew, Mark, Luke, John and the stories of Joseph and Moses. I did not even know up until 1993 that the Bible is called the Word of God. I was ignorant about the nature and the ways of God. I was puzzled by the fact that God the Father would visit me and things began to happen in my life that made me to end up in the psychiatric hospital a few days afterwards. I had a lot of questions and I needed answers.

I was so determined to find out what had happened to me and to find out why I could be so blessed and yet be so horribly afflicted. I took a six month leave of absence and went to Nigeria and true to His Word, God delivered me and began to give me revelations about

Himself in His Word and also revelations about the devil. During the times that the devil was tormenting me, I would see him raging and pointing his finger at me while telling me all the evil things that he was going to do to me. I would be so surprised at his anger because I was so sure that he did not know me and I did not know what I had done to him to make him so angry. I had six months of intense Bible study Monday through Friday from 9 am to 5 pm.

When I came back from Nigeria, my whole perspective in life changed and I decided that I wanted to use the rest of my life to serve God. I realized that I had lived without God for so long that now that He has apprehended me, I too was going try to apprehend Him and know Him. Besides, He made that special effort to come down from heaven to talk to me so my life must therefore be for His glory. Therefore, I gave up my job in New York and I came to Atlanta and I wanted to do things for God but what I had was "zeal without knowledge." I did not ask God about what He wanted me to do but presumptuously started to do "good deeds" for Him. I did this full time for about two years before I gained some wisdom.

I then decided to go back to work and every door that I was trying to get into was shut in my face. Every where I went to apply for a job, they would tell me that they have nothing for me even though I have a master's degree and a wealth of experience. They will then say to me, "We have a position in the Administrative Department." I was shocked at the number of companies that only wanted to push me towards their administrative department for a secretarial position. I said no, no and no to them. I was grieved by what was going on so I went to the Lord and I asked Him, "Why am I being pushed by these people to administrative positions even after they read my resume? They look at what I have done and it is as though they do not even pay attention and they see me as fit for only administrative positions."

It was ridiculous to be offered an administrative position with my qualification and work experience. The Lord said to me, "It is because of the covenant that your mother made on your behalf concerning employment. That was her desire for you. Remember when she wanted you to be a secretary to her manager?" I was in shocked because that was something that happened so many years ago. He said to me, "If you forgive your mother and renounce that covenant that she made with that man that you are to be his secretary, then I will drive away the spirit." I prayed and I forgave my mother and I renounced the covenant. Not long after, I got a job and it still started as an administrative position but the Lord told me to take it so that He could deliver me out of it.

Not long after, the Lord opened my eyes to see Him remove from inside of me, the old Pitman Typewriter that had been embedded in me. I then remembered that my mother had said "NO" to my going to high school when I finished elementary school. She had actually enrolled me in a typing school where they were using an old Pitman typewriter because she could not afford to pay for high school for me and my brother at the same time. However, God made a way and with the help of a twelve year-old little boy, I secretly began to go to high school without her knowledge! I was so glad to see the Holy Spirit yank that old ugly typewriter out of me and I watched as He threw it away.

Many parents do not understand the power of the words that they speak over their children; even the words that they speak over their children's future in areas of marriage, employment, success in life, favor, health, etc. A parent's ungodly words (words that are not in line with God's plan for the child) over his or her child can lock the child up in life because they are not God's plans for the child. Just like what happened to me, a parent's ungodly words or confessions over a child can hinder the child every time the child wants to move in the area that God had prepared for him or her. The ungodly words spoken by the parent then become the legal ground that the devil uses to hinder the child from having success or prosperity in life. These are some of the legalities and the technicalities that the devil uses to hinder people in life. I am going to discuss these in detail in Chapter 3 of this book. Therefore, I say to parents, do not speak something that is not in line with God's Word, God's plan and purpose over your children. If you do, you will make it impossible for them to succeed in life because your ungodly words will always conflict with God's plan for them. They become the ace card in the devil's hand against them.

The Ungodly Covenant by the Children of Israel:

If we do not take the time to properly understand the power of covenant, we can become like the children of Israel in the days of Joshua. In **Joshua 9:3**, we see Joshua and the children of Israel about to make a covenant with their enemies. It is actually an evil covenant but as I stated before, our God is a God of covenant and if you make a covenant with the devil, that covenant binds you until the day that you choose to get yourself out of it or until someone in your family rises up in righteousness and says no to it. According to the scriptures, Joshua and the children of Israel came into the land of Canaan and they gained victory over Jericho and Ai but they had enemies —the Gibeonites and these Gibeonites lived in the area that the children of Israel occupied. The Gibeonites understood the power of covenants and they also know something about the God of Israel; they knew that He is a God of covenant. Therefore, they knew that if they can get the children of Israel to cut a covenant with them in the name of their God, they would keep the children of Israel from making war with them and annihilating them. We can see how they disguised themselves and set out to make this covenant with the children of Israel in **Joshua 9:3-16:**

> **"And when the inhabitants of Gibeon heard what Joshua had done unto Jericho and to Ai, *4* They did work wilily, and went and made as if they had been ambassadors, and took old sacks upon their asses, and wine bottles, old, and rent, and bound up;** *(They are trying to trick Joshua and the children of Israel.)* **5 And old shoes and clouted upon their feet, and old garments upon them; and all the bread of their provision was dry and mouldy. *6* And they went to Joshua unto the camp at Gilgal, and**

said unto him, and to the men of Israel, We be come from a far country: now therefore make ye a league with us.** *(In other words, cut a covenant with us and come into agreement with us.)* **7 And the men of Israel said unto the Hivites, Peradventure ye dwell among us; and how shall we make a league with you?** *(So there was a check in their spirit that these people might not be all that they are claiming to be but they did not investigate to find out.)* **8 And they said unto Joshua, We are thy servants. And Joshua said unto them, Who are ye? and from whence come ye? 9 And they said unto him, <u>From a very far country thy servants are come because of the name of the LORD thy God</u>:** *(You see, they know something about God.)* <u>**for we have heard the fame of him, and all that he did in Egypt,**</u> **10 And all that he did to the two kings of the Amorites, that were beyond Jordan, to Sihon king of Heshbon, and to Og king of Bashan, which was at Ashtaroth. 11 Wherefore our elders and all the inhabitants of our country spake to us, saying, Take victuals with you for the journey, and go to meet them, and say unto them, <u>We are your servants: therefore now make ye a league with us</u>.** *(Cut a covenant with us.)* **12 This our bread we took hot for our provision out of our houses on the day we came forth to go unto you; but now, behold, it is dry, and it is mouldy: 13 And these bottles of wine, which we filled, were new; and, behold, they be rent: and these our garments and our shoes are become old by reason of the very long journey.** *(They were lying to the children of Israel by trying to make them believe that they were from a country far away whereas they were their neighbors.)* **14 <u>And the men took of their victuals, and asked not counsel at the mouth of the LORD</u>. 15 And <u>Joshua made peace with them,</u> and <u>made a league with them,</u> <u>to let them live</u>: and the princes of the congregation sware unto them.**

> *16* **And it came to pass at the end of three days after they had made a league with them, that they heard that they were their neighbours**, and that they dwelt among them."

The children of Israel knew that they had to honor the covenant because they made it in the name of the Lord. Although this covenant was not a good covenant for the children of Israel, it was a valid covenant as far as God was concerned because it was made in His name. God's commandment through Moses was for the children of Israel to destroy the Gibeonites but as a result of the covenant, the children of Israel could not destroy the Gibeonites. This covenant was in place during the time of King Saul and King David. King Saul's actions against the Gibeonites brought a "three-year famine" upon the land of Israel because he violated this covenant by rising up against the Gibeonites. He killed many of them because he did not understand the power of a covenant from God's perspective. Although King Saul violated the covenant with the Gibeonites during his life time, the famine happened after his death and during the reign of King David. When King David inquired from the Lord in **2 Samuel 21:1** concerning the famine, the Lord said it was because Saul violated the covenant with the Gibeonites:

> "Then **there was a famine in the days of David three years**, year after year; and David enquired of the LORD. **And the LORD answered, It is for Saul**, and **for his bloody house, because he slew the Gibeonites**."

It makes you wonder about some of the negative things that we are dealing with today that might be the consequences of the ungodly actions of the generations before us. When King David wanted to know from the Gibeonites what he could do to appease them, the Gibeonites knew that King Saul had seventy sons and they asked for all their heads! All seventy sons of King Saul were killed and their heads were delivered to the Gibeonites so that the curse of famine would be removed from the land of Israel. What this story about

Joshua, the children of Israel and King Saul's actions tells us is that we should be very careful about the covenants that we cut because if we mistakenly make a covenant with the devil, all we do is tie God's hands from moving on our behalf because He respects covenants. This should also make you wonder about what covenant you and your family members may have violated that has been producing negative effects in your lives. Covenants are powerful and they last forever unless otherwise specified.

How God Views the Marriage Covenant:

The following story is a case in point of how God views covenants and what He taught me about the marriage covenant:

> *There was a young man that used to work with me when I first started out in ministry. He had just got out of prison but while he was in prison, he got saved. Not long after he got out of prison and was working with me, he met a young lady at one of the local convenient stores. I guess he did not want to fornicate with her so he decided to jump into marriage. When he did not show up for work for three days, I became very concerned and began to wonder about what may have happened to him. It was unlike him not to call or show up for work so I asked the Lord what was going on with him. The Lord told me that he had eloped with the young lady he recently met and the Lord told me that when he comes back, I should leave him alone because He (the Lord) respects the marriage covenant and I should do the same. He told me not to speak good or bad against the marriage. The Lord knew that I was aware that the girl was not the right person for him but the Lord said I must honor the covenant. Not quite three months after the marriage, he wanted out of the marriage because of the manifestations that*

> *he was seeing in his new bride at night! I just simply told him to seek the Lord for deliverance but I did not say a word about what he had done or what I thought about the marriage.*

Since this incident, I only talk to people concerning the mate that they are about to choose before they go into a marriage covenant because once they cut that covenant, I have to respect the covenant because God respects the covenant. It may be the biggest mistake of their lives but a covenant is a covenant.

This is also the reason why I have to educate people about covenants when they come up to me and say that they have been married for years before becoming saved but they now realize that the marriage was a mistake and they need for me to seek God's will. I simply tell them that God is a God of covenant and that He honored their marriage covenant; just because the marriage got off track and the love has fizzled away does not mean that the covenant is no longer valid. If you are one of such people, what you need to do is ask the Lord to bring back the love in your relationship because God can do anything if you are willing and obedient. He will help you to uphold your marriage covenant. You cannot go to God and say, "Oh God, when I married my spouse, I really was not in love with him/her but I have now found someone that I truly love so I want out of my marriage." It does not work that way; if you are married, you have to honor your marriage covenant and not bail out when you think the grass is greener on the other side. Many men are leaving their wives of many years for younger women. Tell me, why God will not judge them for being covenant breakers?

There are a lot of divorce cases today because people are now getting married for convenience and the fact that they cut a marriage covenant has become irrelevant. They do not understand the power of covenant so when they marry someone and things do not work out for them immediately and if there is any distress or if she does not look the way she used to look, they immediately break their marriage covenant. Some will set aside their marriage when the financial status of their spouse changes. If the spouse can no longer provide for them as in time past, they immediately begin to look for a greener pasture else where. These types of people are living dangerously with God because God Himself judges covenant breakers; especially those who break the marriage covenant.

The Future Fate of Covenant Breakers:

When you read **Romans 1:29-32**, you will see that God plans to judge all those who engage in what we call the sin of the flesh. Listed among the people to be judge by God are covenant breakers:

> "**Being filled with all unrighteousness, fornication, wickedness, covetousness, maliciousness; full of envy, murder, debate, deceit, malignity; whisperers, *30* Backbiters, haters of God, despiteful, proud, boasters, inventors of evil things, disobedient to parents, *31* Without understanding, <u>covenantbreakers</u>, without natural affection, implacable, unmerciful: *32* <u>Who knowing the judgment of God, that they which commit such things are worthy of death</u>, <u>not only do the same, but have pleasure in them that do them</u>.**"

Because we do not understand how God honors covenants and how powerful covenants are in Christendom, our actions concerning covenants are either preventing God from moving on our behalf or they are allowing the devil to operate in our lives. Many of us do not understand the true meaning of our salvation so there are some people that believe that once you are saved, everything in your life is taken care of and you do not have to ask for anything and all generational curses are taken care of. They will persecute you when you start preaching on generational curses and they will tell you that such things do not exist but when you look at them, they are in every prayer line for financial breakthrough, a job, relationships and deliverance from sickness and diseases.

My question to such people is, "How come all these things did not just line up in your life when you became born again?" The fact remains that when you became born again, if you had ten dollars in your bank account, it will still remain ten dollars the next day and if your spouse was angry with you, he or she was still angry with you when you got home. The reason is because when you got born again, the salvation you received was in your human spirit. Our human spirit was recreated in the image of God's Son by God's Spirit and we became of a higher birth. This is why Jesus said in **Matthew 11:11:**

"Verily I say unto you, Among them that are born of women there hath not risen a greater than John the Baptist: <u>notwithstanding he that is least in the kingdom of heaven</u> *(the least believer)* **<u>is greater than he</u>."**

The Lord said that John the Baptist was **the greatest among all that are born of women** but the least believer in the Kingdom of God is greater than John the Baptist. This means that if John the Baptist is the highest in the old covenant, we that are in the new covenant are greater than him. **The reason is because we are born of the Spirit of God and this is a higher birth than that of John who is born of a woman!** This higher birth entitles us to God's covenant blessings.

Understanding How God's Kingdom is Set Up:

We have to really understand how God has set up His kingdom and how the kingdom operates so that we can maximize the kingdom blessings and benefits for ourselves. This is what happened at our new birth. At our new birth, God came into our human spirit and recreated our human spirit and He deposited His Holy Spirit into us to begin to guide us and help us understand scriptures. The Holy Spirit also helps us get information from God and He takes our prayers and petitions to God but when it comes to our mind, it is our responsibility to renew our mind with the Word of God. God will not accomplish this for us but He will give us the grace to understand His Word when we choose to read it. We have to read the Word of God and change our thought patterns to line up with it.

The devil is no dummy; he knows that your spirit is saved and that he cannot have access to it. As a result, he targets two places in your life —your mind and your body! He knows the scripture that says "as a man thinks, so is he" **(Proverbs 23:7)** and as a result, he wants you to think wrong thoughts so that you can do the wrong things. Also, he knows that a physically dead Christian cannot contend with him here on earth so he will try to attack your body. Therefore, you cannot neglect your God-given responsibilities concerning your mind and your body. You cannot allow the devil access to them by being ignorant about the power of covenants. The following story shows how the devil is eager to get believers out of the earth and how he tried to get me to choose death.

A few years ago, I was coming back to the US from Africa and as soon the plane took off, the devil said to me, "Whether you live or die, you belong to the Lord; what does it matter if you live or die." He began to sell me on the idea of how fascinating a plane tumbling down in a crash would be. He wanted me to regarded it as the ultimate thrill but I said to him, "It is expedient for me to be alive because I have to do things for the Lord, so get off and be gone." I immediately declared that I choose life and not death. While this was going on, the plane hit a great turbulence and began to turn almost belly up! The luggage compartments swung open and people were screaming as the plane seemed to be spinning out of control. I rebuked the spirit of death and destruction and I again declared that I choose to live and not die. I remembered how the devil tried to get me into an agreement with him before it all began. I declared to the Lord that I choose to remain here on earth so that I can finish my destiny and I reminded Him that He needs me right here on earth because this is where I can do something for the kingdom. I told Him that when I get to heaven, I cannot do something for Him concerning winning souls. He gave me the wisdom to command the plane to be still and I yelled, "Peace, be still!" The plane immediately began to get back into its proper alignment and the pilot seemed to be regaining control of the plane and everything became calm again.

We the believers can do a lot for God's kingdom here on earth. Therefore, the devil comes in and he tries to sidetrack us either through false visions and false dreams or through words that will get us into a covenant agreement with him so that he can effectively attack or kill us using our own covenant agreement with him. This is why you have to be very discerning in what you hear because hearing a voice does not mean that the voice is from God. You have to know the voice of God so that you can tell when the devil is trying to deceive you. What the voices you hear say to you must always line up with the Word of God.

As I stated in one of my books titled, **Keys to Understanding Your Visions and Dreams** (pages 59-60), you have to test every spirit to make sure that it is from God before you come into an agreement with it. The following story is an example of what I am warning you against. It shows how the devil can use a word to deceive a person.

Excerpt:

> *There was a lady that used to call Pastor Jonas. The lady was a Christian who had converted to Islam. This is how the devil can use a word, a vision or a dream to deceive a person. Pastor Jonas talked with her for months until he was tired of the conversations. Knowing that I was delivered from a Muslim background, he referred her to me, hoping that she would listen to me.*
>
> *I discovered that she grew up in a Pentecostal home and I asked her how she became a Muslim. She said she was praying one day and went into the woods to meditate (she had learned eastern meditation). While there, she received a word but did not know what it meant. The word sounded Arabic. Not knowing what to do,*

she went into a phone booth to call someone for help in understanding the word. The first page she turned to in the telephone directory had a word that was similar to the word she had received. She called the number and it was a Muslim phone listing. She told them that she wanted to get an understanding of the word. Of course, they were more than glad to oblige her. They went to her house with Islamic books. Within a few months, they changed her name to a Muslim name and began the initiation process to convert her from Christianity to Islam.

Now, she challenges everything in the Bible because her Muslim teachers taught her that mere men wrote the Bible and that it has several different versions whose meanings do not all agree and she believed them. She also believed her teachers when they told her that Jesus never referred to Himself as the Son of God and that the disciples made up all of their accounts. The devil got her with a "spooky spiritual" word!

I told her that Jesus said, "I am the Word, the Truth and the Life and no man comes to the Father but by Me." I informed her that she became derailed from the Way, the Truth and the Life when she got her interpretation through the phone book instead of the Bible. I also told her that when she went into the woods to do eastern meditation, she opened her mind up to the devil through the meditation, and allowed him to speak to her. The devil spoke a word that he knew would mislead her; and her ignorance landed her right in the laps of the Muslims.

This lady was once on fire for the Lord and it took the devil one word to get her to side track and fall away. She fell into the devil's trap because she had an evil covenant with the spirit of "eastern meditation." You do not go to the woods and just empty your mind through eastern meditation because if you do, the devil will send his spirits into your mind. The devil loves a vacuum and when you create a vacuum in your mind through eastern meditation, he will help you to fill it. The Bible never told the believer to empty his or her mind but rather, it says to fill our mind with the Word of God. Our meditation is to repeat the Word of God —say it to yourself over and over until you work it into your spirit and until it births a revelation in you. That is the type of meditation that we are to practice but not eastern meditation that involves yoga and that leaves your mind blank because many want to transcend their human bodies. They want to go to another spiritual level that is above their earthly bodies because they believe that the body is not what really matters so they want to involve into another spiritual level. This is heresy because God gave you a body so that you can relate to the material world that you live in. It is what makes you human! What God wants on earth is a man —a true human being (man or woman) and not some spooky being without a human body.

If you are a Christian, you do not get involved in eastern yoga or eastern meditations because if you do, it becomes a covenant with the devil. When we look at our lives today, we find that many of our relatives have made covenants on our behalf from past generations; especially when you look the present generation. Since the 1960s, many people have developed the mind set of self ownership. Their belief is that "it is my life and I can do whatever I want to do with it and it is nobody else's business." The result is that when you look at young people today, it seems as if the world is being turned upside down by their beliefs and ways of life. What they are not aware of is the spiritual truth that your life is not just your life because whatever you do today is going to impact the generations after you. You will either leave a legacy of blessings or curses for them based on your actions and way of life!

Chapter 2

Understanding How God Uses Covenants

Today, we praise and worship God with songs and dance and many other forms that depict our love and reverence of Him. We can do these things and God is pleased to receive them because we are a people that have a covenant with Him. The Bible says that we have a better covenant with God than the one the children of Israel had with Him. The Lord Jesus mediated this better covenant for us with His own blood on Calvary. This is why **Hebrews 8:6** says:

> **"But now hath he obtained a more excellent ministry, by how much also <u>he is the mediator of a better covenant, which was established upon better promises</u>."**

Sometimes we read a scripture and we do not stop to really ponder what the scripture is saying to us. Most times, it takes God to help us understand it even though we read it all the time. The above scripture is one of such scriptures that we cannot afford to just glaze over. As we saw in Chapter one, we have a very unique relationship with God through the Everlasting Covenant that the Lord Jesus established with His own blood. Many of us have had visions in which we saw either God the Father, God the Son or God the Holy Spirit. Some of us see into the heavenly and particularly into the throne room every day or every week. Many have conversations with the Lord on a daily basis. All these are great and wonderful for us as believers but when we stop to think about the type of relationship that those who were under the law had with God, we have to sing the song *Amazing Grace*. The Lord Jesus Himself said it in **Luke 10: 23-24:**

> **"And <u>he turned him unto his disciples, and said privately</u>, Blessed are the eyes which see the things that ye see: *24* For I tell you, that many prophets and kings have desired to see those things which**

ye see, and have not seen them; and to hear those things which ye hear, and have not heard them."

We daily enjoy the presence of the Lord and the benefits of seeing Him or hearing His voice. These are demonstrations of the better covenant and better promises that we have with God. The Lord showed me how better our covenant with Him is when He led me to Exodus 33. Moses had been leading the children of Israel through the wilderness for years when he suddenly realized something critical. He realized that when God is with you, your life will never be the same and that **when you have the presence of the Lord, you become unbeatable no matter where you are.** Therefore, Moses began to desire the PRESENCE of the Lord and in **Exodus 33:13** he says to the Lord:

> "Now therefore, I pray thee, **if I have found grace in thy sight, shew me now thy way, that I may know thee, that I may find grace in thy sight:** and consider that this nation is thy people."

In response God said to him in **Exodus 33:14:**

> "…**My presence shall go with thee**, and I will give thee rest."

Moses does not stop there. He is hungry for the manifested presence (glory) of God and he says in **Exodus 33:15-16**:

> "And he said unto him, **If thy presence go not with me, carry us not up hence.** For wherein shall it be known here that I and thy people have **found grace in thy sight**?"

If you drop down to **verse 18,** you will see what Moses is really asking for. He wants to behold the glory of the Lord.

> "And he said, I beseech thee, **shew me thy glory.**"

It is one thing to be in the presence of the Lord but it is another thing to experience the glory of the Lord. Moses is aware of this so he asked for more revelation of being in the presence of the Lord. He said, "Show me your glory." Then the Lord said to him in **Exodus 33:19**:

> **"And he said, <u>I will make all my goodness pass before thee</u>, and <u>I will proclaim the name of the LORD before thee</u>; and will be gracious to whom I will be gracious, and will show mercy on whom I will show mercy."**

In other words, God is saying to Moses, I will let you see my goodness and I will tell you my name. I will even let you know how I judge **but I will not let you see my face because of where you are**.

> **"And he said, <u>Thou canst not see my face</u>: for <u>there</u>** *(a place)* **<u>shall no man see me, and live</u>"** (Exodus 33:20).

We that are born again take it for granted that we are freely able to behold God's glory and even the Lord Jesus prayed to God the Father in **John 17:24** that we might behold His glory!

> **"Father, <u>I will that they also, whom thou hast given me, be with me where I am; that they may behold my glory</u>, which thou hast given me: for thou lovedst me before the foundation of the world."**

The reason that we can behold His glory today is because of the better covenant that the Lord mediated for us. We are in Christ, "The Rock" but when you read the beginning of Exodus Chapter 33, you will see that Moses was in the **tabernacle of the congregation or the outer court. It is true that no one who operates in the outer court can see God and live because they will only see Him as their judge**. If you see God in the outer court, you will die because you are not sanctified unto Him by the blood of His Son, Jesus. In the outer court, you are not renewed, you are still carnal minded, you are ruled by your flesh and you do not have the Spirit of God inside of you. As a result, you cannot get into the Holy of Holies or the Most Holy Place where God is. It takes sanctification by the blood of Jesus, purity of heart and a life of holiness to behold God. This is why Jesus said, "Blessed are the pure in heart for they shall see God." Purity of heart is the result of the sanctification work (renewing of mind and heart) of the Holy Spirit in your life after you are born again.

Therefore, God says to Moses, where you are right now is not the place that you can see Me and live to tell about it. A lot of people have perverted this scripture because the devil has a false doctrine out there that says that "no man can see God and live" but God was talking about the place and position that Moses was in the kingdom. He is talking about the place where He told Moses to meet Him which was in the tabernacle of the congregation. We the believers are seated together with Christ according to **Ephesians 2:6** and we meet with the Lord in the Holy of Holies and before the Throne of Grace **(Hebrews 4:16)**.

Because Moses is not in the place were he can see God and live, God says to him in **Exodus 33:21-23** that there is a place by Him—a Rock where you can see Him and live:

> **"And the LORD said, Behold, <u>there is a place by me</u>,** *(gives you an idea of where is talking about)* **and thou shalt stand upon a rock:** *(who is that rock? Jesus)* **<u>And it shall come to pass, while my glory passeth by, that I will put thee in a clift of the rock</u>** *(again speaking of Jesus)* **<u>and will cover thee with my hand while I pass by</u>: And I will take away mine hand, <u>and thou shalt see my back parts: but my face shall not be seen</u>."**

God refused to show Moses His face. The only place that you can see God's Face and live is in that ROCK OF AGES CALLED JESUS CHRIST! This is why God the Father clothes us with Christ when we become born again. Anybody who would see God's face outside of Christ will never live because they will only see God coming as the judge of their sinful life style. They will never survive the judgment in the outer court because they never lived a holy life, they were never sanctified unto God in their ways and actions and they are not inside the Rock. This is the mass judgment that is going to come upon the world and those who claim to be saved but lived all their lives in the outer court instead of in the Holy of Holies.

Remember what the scripture says in **Hebrews 12:14** that **without holiness no man shall see God?** We the believers are sanctified (set apart) in Christ unto God and we also have to further sanctify ourselves by making righteous choices and walking in the things that do not defile the human spirit in order to see God. Moses was not born again and so could not even begin the process of true sanctification as a result. Therefore, in order for Moses to see anything about God, God had to hide Moses in a Rock. This is that Moses that the Bible says knows the ways of God but he never saw God's face. All he truly had was a glimpse of the back of God and to even see this, God had to hide him in the cleft of the rock —**"I will put thee in the clift of the rock and I will cover thee with my hand while I pass by: And I will take away mine hand, and thou shalt see my back parts: but my face shall not be seen."** Again, God had to do this because Moses was not born again but we the believers are in the Rock because we are in Christ. He is the Rock that God is talking about. Also, we have chosen not to be carnally minded but to think righteously and live holy. The Bible says in **Romans 8:6** that, **"For to be carnally minded is death…"** It was not until the Lord Jesus died and rose again that all who where in the bosom of Abraham; Moses included were freed from where they were kept until the atonement by the blood of Jesus was accomplished. We should all thank God for the better covenant and promises that the Lord mediated for us.

How many of you have beheld the face of the Father, of the Lord Jesus and of the Holy Spirit? Because we are in Christ Jesus, we go into the Holy of Holies and we can behold the face of the Father, the Son and the Holy Spirit. So, you see that this covenant we have with the Lord is a much better covenant than the one that the children of Israel had. What Moses cried out for and was denied of is freely given to us in Christ. As a result, we are able to come before the throne of grace today crying, "Abba, Father." Again, we can feel His presence and behold His glory and interact with Him as His children. We can behold the Father, behold Jesus and behold the Holy Spirit. Why? Because we are dead *(the old man)* and only alive in Christ; we are hidden in Christ. This is why the Bible says concerning us:

"For ye are dead, and your life is hid with Christ in God" (Colossians 3:3).

We are in the cleft of the rock; that is why the Bible also says in **1 Corinthians 6:17** that we are joined unto the Lord —**"But he that is joined unto the Lord is one spirit."** Also, **"We are members of his body, of his flesh, and of his bones** (Ephesians 5:30). Therefore, we are one with Him. We never want to take this covenant with Him for granted; we never want to take what God has given us for granted because it is an awesome privilege. Angels in heaven look at us and go, "Wow, these beings that God so loved that He gave everything for; they have access to Him in a way that no other creation has access to Him." They marvel at the love that God has for us and what He is willing to do for us. We can go before the throne and give God a hug because He is our Father but no angel can do that. We can go and sit on God's lap and God can come into our home or dreams and become our teacher. He treats everyone of us as though we are the most important person in the whole world because to Him, we are. He patiently talks to us and corrects us and the angels just wonder what in the world He sees in these people that can not even do right. He does this because He made a covenant with us in Abraham and in Christ and He loves us.

What makes us the church today is the covenant that we have with God through His Son, Jesus and what made the Jews the people of God is the covenant that they have with Him through Abraham. Today, both the church and the Jews are partakers of the **Abrahamic**

Covenant. God humbled Himself and decided one day that He was going to get Himself some children; He was going to be a Father. He wanted to have a family and to enjoy a family life with His children. This was the desire that led Him to bring us (the Church) to Him through a covenant with His Son and because we are His children and part of Christ, we can enjoy the benefits of sonship. As a result, there are some things that God is obligated to do for us because of the nature and terms of the Abrahamic Covenant and the Everlasting Covenant in the blood of Jesus that He has with us. I have already established the facts that covenants are very critical and that they are very vital in God's kingdom and also that God does not operate outside of covenant.

The next step is to understand how to operate the covenant that we are partaking of. This means that we have to know the way that God wants us to operate His covenant in our lives. There are some things that you invoke using the covenant with the Lord and you immediately get a response. I have had the Lord say to me several times when I invoke His terms of the covenant, "You've made your point." When things get really critical or overwhelming, I will just tell Him as I break bread, "Father, I have a covenant with You and by the terms of this covenant, I am the seed of Abraham today in Christ. You have said… and You placed Yourself under the curse of death if it does not happen, so I am here invoking this covenant today." I say again that a lot of times He goes, "You've made your point." I will then see the results just like that because I have learned from Him how to operate the covenant. Unless what I am asking for is something that He has sovereignty set an appointed time for, I will get a response from Him. It might be clarity about what He is doing in the situation but He will respond. I would like to issue a caution here.

Caution: *This does not mean that you are to threaten God or be rude to Him but that you respectfully remind Him of what He promised concerning your particular situation. Also, before you start invoking covenants with God, you have to know the terms of the covenants. You have to know what God is obligated to do for you and what is your part* *or role according to the terms of the covenants. God is not legalist but He hates ignorance. Therefore, know the terms of the covenants because you do not want Him to say to you,* **"Who is this that darkeneth counsel by words without knowledge?"** (Job 38:2).

I said in a couple of paragraphs above that there are some things that God is obligated to do for us because of the nature and terms of the covenants that He has with us. I repeat that we were brought into the **Abrahamic Covenant** through the **Everlasting Covenant** that the Lord Jesus established with us in His own blood. These two covenants entitle us to some major benefits with God. Let us now look at some of them.

Divine Presence:

After we become born again, we can enjoy the PRESENCE of the Lord. God said to us in Christ Jesus, **"Lo, I am with you always; even to the end of the world.** As I showed you through the scripture in Exodus 33, Moses asked for God's PRESENCE (God's glory; God's face) and He never got it. The best that he got was the back part of God the Father; even then, God put His hand on him, placed him in the rock and only removed His hand after He had gone past Moses! By the time Moses was allowed to look, God was gone far away and Moses was only able to see a glimpse of His back. I have had many visitations from the Lord Jesus and even the Holy Ghost and on May 18, 1993, God the Father walked into my bedroom. He talked with me for about six hours! I still see Him because He is my Father and He is the only Father that I have ever truly known. I see the Lord Jesus and the Holy Ghost as well. It is all part of our covenant blessings in Christ.

My parents were divorced when I was about three or four years old and my brother and I were given to our grandparents but the cry of my heart as a child was to one day just see what my dad looked like. This did not happen until I was about eleven years old but I did not get to spend time with him. I resented my dad for many years because he walked away from us without looking back but when I became born again, I forgave him. I then had this desire to spend just one day alone with my dad or to spend just one day alone with both my mom and dad at the same time but my dad died before my next visit home. God the Father has truly fulfilled my heart's desire to have a father. Since I became born again, He became the Father that I never had and I know that the reason this happens is because of the covenant that I have with Him through the blood of Jesus.

Because divine presence is given to us by God, we have to know that it is not something that we have to pray for and cry for anymore. His desire is to be part of our lives and to be with us and as a result, divine presence is given to us freely. The Lord Jesus said that **"...Where two or three are gathered together in my name, there am I in the midst of them!"**(Matthew 18:20). It is true that God is everywhere (Omnipresent) but the manifested presence of God is not everywhere because only those who are in a covenant relationship with the Him will experience it. Therefore, I am shocked when Christians come together to pray or worship and they begin to cry and pray for God's presence to come. This is ignorance because all we have to do is acknowledge that His presence is in our midst and we will free Him up to take us to another level in Him. We need to stop praying for what has been freely given to us already and just learn to receive it.

Many people will never be able to experience the presence of the Lord because they have not obeyed His Word to come into a covenant relationship with Him. I remember when I use to preach the Gospel over the phone and we would go through the white pages of the phone book and call people up and preach the Gospel to them and I called it telemarketing the Gospel. Although we did not charge any fees or talk about money with the people but just call them up and preach the Gospel to them, some people did like the term telemarketing the Gospel. As far as I was concerned, we were reaching very many people with the Gospel over the phone.

During one of those calls, I happened to have called someone who was a Muslim and I started talking to him about the Lord. I explained to him the difference between Jesus and Mohammed; how that Jesus rose again and is alive and Mohammed is dead and buried. I told him that Jesus was alive and talks to His children and that we can ask Him a question and He will give us an answer and that Mohammed cannot do that. His next question led us to the topic of divine visitation and divine presence and I remember how shocked he was to hear that we can see Jesus. He said, "Anybody who has seen Jesus or seen God needs to be on CNN." He said this because he was not part of the covenant that believers have with God, it seemed to him an impossible thing for someone to see the Lord Jesus or God the Father. We should never take God's divine presence for granted and we should not show our ignorance of the terms of the covenant by petitioning God to do what He already does every time we come together.

We also receive deliverance in God's divine presence. For instance, if you need to feel the presence of the Lord (because He is in you) and because you are in a place in which you are feeling very oppressed, all you have to say is, "Father as a joint heir with Christ, I know that You are with me and that Your presence is with me but I need to feel it right now. Thank you that it is part of the benefits of the covenant that I have with You in Christ." You will be surprised at the Lord's response to you because He loves it when He sees us apprehend His kingdom principles. He loves it when we are operating in His wisdom because He does not like ignorance. The minute that you begin to know how to operate the terms of His covenant agreement, He will begin to work with you so that you can grow in applying the principles. There are times that I have said something or done something while invoking the covenant and He will give me a clap of approval.

This is just to let you know how God appreciates those who know what He has done for them already. One day, I was in a service and the congregation was singing the song, "***God Prepare Me to be a Sanctuary.***" I said to the Lord, forgive us for not accepting what you have already done for us because you have already made us **"Sanctuaries of Your Holy Spirit."** I then began to sing, **"God, you've made me your sanctuary that is pure and holy; that is** tried and true..." He immediately responded by pouring out a hot anointing upon me and said, "This is what I am talking about; those who know who they are." Therefore, we all must recognize what God has already done for us and walk in it.

Divine Protection:

The next thing God promised is divine protection. As the seed of Abraham in Christ, God's promises of protection to us are:

> "**And I will bless them that bless thee, and curse him that curseth thee**: and in thee shall all families of the earth be blessed" (Genesis 12:3).

> "**There shall no evil befall thee, neither shall any plague come nigh thy dwelling**" (Psalm 91:10).

> "**For ye shall go out with joy, and be led forth with peace**: the mountains and the hills shall break forth before you into singing, and all the trees of the field shall clap their hands. *13* Instead of the thorn shall come up the fir tree, and instead of the brier shall come up the myrtle tree" (Isaiah 55:12-13).

Also, the Lord Jesus told us in **John 10:29** that we are in the Father's hand and that no one is able to pluck us away from the Father's hand:

> "**My Father, which gave them me, is greater than all; and no man is able to pluck them out of my Father's hand.**"

God also promised to fight for us in **Isaiah 49:25**. Anyone that wants to contend with us will have to answer to God because He will personally contend with the person:

> "...for **I will contend with him that contendeth with thee**, and I will save thy children."

And in **Psalm 89:23** He also promised to beat down our enemies and to plague those that hate us:

"And <u>I will beat down his foes before his face</u>, and <u>plague them that hate him</u>."

There are times when these scriptures above have helped me to get out of trouble. When I go to a place and I am feeling oppressed by the spirits in the people or the place, I would say, "Lord, I thank you for your covenant of protection. I am being oppressed right now and there are spirits trying to plague me so I invoke the covenant of protection that I have with You and I need Your divine instruction." One time, He told me, "Command the fire of the Holy Ghost upon you to the intent that it will burn up the evil things that are trying to attach themselves to you." In obedience I said, "I command the fire of the Holy Ghost and the wrath and fury of God upon me to burn up and destroy everything that has risen up against me but let the mercy and goodness of God follow me all the days of my life." The oppression immediately lifted!

Praise God for His covenant of protection with us. If you know how to walk in God's covenant of protection, you will not go to a place and come back afflicted nor will people visit you and deposit wicked or lingering spirits around you or your home to vex you. With some people, all the devil has to do is send someone with a vexing spirit to speak with them on the phone and for the rest of the day, their minds are scrambled; they are unable to focus because the spirit is vexing their soul. Therefore, we need to understand the protection God has already given us and know how to apply it with His wisdom. God said to me one day, **"When I send you somewhere, do not be afraid to get into trouble on my account because if I allow you to get in trouble, you better believe that I am God enough to deliver you."** Therefore, when God sends me to a place, I am not afraid of the place or the people in it because I know that God is with me.

Jesus told us that God so protects and cares for us that even the very hairs on our heads are numbered. Not one hair will fall to the ground without God knowing about it.

"But the very hairs of your head are all numbered" (Matthew 10:30).

There are some spiritual principles that are applicable to both the Old and the New Covenants. Apprehending a thief and taking back what was stolen are part of those principles because God hates stealing and He encourages His children to take back what was stolen from them. This should be an encouragement to the men that are loosing their hair. If you are one of such men, you should use this covenant promise to ask for divine protection of your hair and there is also a scripture that you can use to claim divine restitution. It is in **Exodus 22:7** and it says, **"If the thief be found, let him pay double"** so pick up that strand of hair and say, "Lord, this is evidence; I apprehended the thief of hair loss right now and I need two strands of hairs for every strand that I have lost." Watch the Lord restore your hair in double if you say this in sincere faith. This is why we have to know how to apply the covenant promises so that we can walk in the fullness of our covenant blessings and inheritance. A lot of men and women are losing their hair and they are not demanding restoration from the devil. Hair loss is part of the result of the fall that was orchestrated by the devil against Adam and his descendants. This therefore should be a major hint to the men and women that have not exercised their right in this area. Command the devil to restore the hair that he stole from you.

Divine Empowerment:

Divine empowerment is another thing that God gives us. Jesus said in **Acts 1:8** that we shall receive power after the Holy Ghost has come upon us in order to be effective witnesses. You received this empowerment when you became filled with the Holy Spirit:

> "**But <u>ye shall receive power, after that the Holy Ghost is come upon you</u>: and ye shall be witnesses unto me both in Jerusalem, and in all Judaea, and in Samaria, and unto the uttermost part of the earth.**"

You cannot be an effective witness if you have not received the baptism of the Holy Spirit and His power. Without the power of the Holy Spirit, you can go to certain places and come back sick because you do not have the grace that will keep you no matter where you are. I remember when we were looking for a building for the ministry and Lisa and I went to look at different houses and buildings. One of the places we went to was the home of an American guy who sold oriental arts. We looked at every room and we also saw all the artworks but as we were walking towards the car, I discern a foul spirit that had attached itself to Lisa from the artworks. I turned to Lisa and said, "A spirit is trying to follow you out of this house from the artwork. Do I have your permission to rebuke it? She gave me permission and I rebuked the foul spirit. I wondered briefly how she picked up the spirit because we entered each room together and the Lord reminded me of what we heard in the house.

The young lady in the house had told us that her mother left her dad and that her dad was selling the house because it had become too big. The Lord then informed me that the spirit from the artwork was just an opportunistic spirit that had tried to latch onto Lisa from the artwork because Lisa had suffered a broken marriage also. The spirit in the artwork was the same spirit that had broken up Lisa's marriage and it was active in the house and was responsible for breaking up the marriage in the house! So, there might be opportunistic spirits in some of the places that you go to and they might try to afflict you but you have to discern them and you have to exercise your covenant right to root them out. They do not have a right to attach themselves to you if you are born again but it is your job to enforce your covenant right. If you are not discerning, you can be on medication for years because of something that you can just rebuke with one word and it goes away.

The Lord Jesus has already given us divine empowerment. If you are born again, you already have it. This means that all believers are already empowered. Now, do we have to pray asking God to give us His power? Some Christians pray this all the time so when I go to a prayer meeting and they are praying such prayers, I just leave because I know that God hates ignorance. You can stir up the power of God that is within you, you can ask the Lord to let the anointing flow but you must know that it is already within you. The day the Holy Ghost took up residence in you as His house, you became endued with power from on high. You are not going to get anymore power but what you are going to get is a release of the power in your life as you learn to walk in God's wisdom and as you grow in the knowledge and ways of God. As this happens, the things that have been hindering or preventing you from moving in that power will begin to drop off your life but as far as the power is concerned you have it already.

Just to give you an idea of the power that God has placed in the believer, it takes at least a thousand demons or more to kill one believer and even then, they still need the help and cooperation through the ungodly words from that believer's mouth! If the believer's words do not agree with the plans of the demons, they will fail because we have so much power; only the words from our mouth have the most power to destroy us. So, divine empowerment is already given to us. The Lord Jesus has given us power over the devil and all his evil spirits. This is recorded in **Luke 10:19:**

"<u>Behold, I give unto you power to tread on serpents and scorpions</u>, and <u>over ALL the power of the enemy</u>: and <u>nothing shall by any means hurt you</u>."

What other power are we looking for when God has already given us all the power we need over the devil and all his evil spirits? These things are already given to us in the new covenant. Therefore, we should learn to exercise the power rather than spend our time praying for God to give us power. Again, I say that you must know what you already have because if you do not know what you have, you are going to be unsure of who you really are and what you can do according to the Word of God. I told you earlier on that God the Father visited me about seven months after I became born again. After He left, the devil also visited me with his lies. As a result of his harassments and lies, I ended in a psychiatric hospital. Because I was not in a spirit filled church and had no spiritual guidance, I could not understand why I was seeing the Lord just about everyday and still have the devil constantly harass me afterwards.

I went back to Nigeria to look for God even though the Lord spoke with me everyday. My pastor in Nigeria knew that I lacked knowledge of the Word of God because I told him that I came to look for God in Nigeria. He replied by telling me that "God is His Word." When I asked him what he meant, he asked me if I had a Bible and when I said yes, he said, "The Bible is the Word of God." I felt really stupid standing before him thinking of how I paid $1,600 to buy a plane ticket to go to Nigeria when all I needed was the Bible! I was assigned someone to teach me the Bible everyday, Monday thru Friday for six months. I learned a lot about who I was in Christ and what had already been given to me by God. I learned spiritual warfare and I came back delivered, bold and strong against the devil.

To further illustrate how ignorant I was about my rights in Christ and who I was in Christ, when I arrived in Nigeria, one of the elders in the church who was also a friend of my mother came up to me and asked me, "Do you have the Holy Ghost?" Mind you that before this time, I had seen God the Father, I saw and still see the Lord Jesus and I had even seen the Holy Spirit but I could not say to her emphatically, "Yes, I have the Holy Spirit." I was not sure of what I had been given because I was afraid of the word "anointing" but I did not want to miss out on anything that I was supposed to have so I said, "Yes, I have the Holy Spirit." My reply was a statement of faith because I was not sure if I had the Holy Spirit or not. She asked me if I was sure because she saw the uncertainty on my face. I thank God for being All-seeing and All-knowing because at my next

Bible study, He decided to help me to become sure of what He had given me.

The next day at my Bible study, the person who had been teaching me the Bible was out of town and a different person came in and he looked at me for a while and said, "Today, I am going to teach you about the Holy Spirit." He took me to **John 14:17** where the Lord Jesus said that the Holy Ghost was going to be with me and in me:

> **"Even the Spirit of truth; whom the world cannot receive, because it seeth him not, neither knoweth him: but ye know him; for he dwelleth with you, and shall be in you."**

And also in **John 14:26**:

> **"But the Comforter, which is the Holy Ghost, whom the Father will send in my name, he shall teach you all things, and bring all things to your remembrance, whatsoever I have said unto you"** (John 14: 26).

Right there, I got delivered of so many things because when the devil first appeared to me, he portrayed himself as the Lord and he began to speak to me and some of the things he told me did not line up scriptures. Even though I did not know scripture, I knew that some of the things he said were very questionable and I was amazed at what I was learning as this person began to teach me about the workings of the Holy Spirit during this Bible study. Also, I had a dramatic visitation by a spirit who told me that I needed to confess my sins; it spoke and acted as if he was from God. As I listened to the teaching in this Bible study, it became clear to me that the spirit was also not the Holy Spirit.

When I left the Bible study, I thanked God for helping me to understand that the spirit that had visited me was a counterfeit spirit and not His Holy Spirit. During the visitation, the spirit showed me that I was waiting to be judged and that I needed to confess my sins. I had spent that whole night confessing my sins to this spirit and for months afterwards, I would go to a corner to confess my sins every time I remembered something that I forgot to confess. This made my early Christian experience very tedious because every time I would finish confessing my sins, I would remember something else that I needed to confess. The agreement and covenant with the counterfeit spirit that I needed to constantly confess my sins, placed me in bondage for a long time. It was quite a relief for me to learn that the Holy Spirit was not the same as the counterfeit spirit so I was able to renounce every agreement and covenant that I had made with it. I learned that the Holy Spirit was the Spirit of GRACE. It was a great deliverance for me because the counterfeit spirit used to challenge every scripture and every Word of God that anyone said to me but as soon as I renounced the agreement and covenant with it, I never heard from it again. Now, I am able to quickly recognize when a counterfeit spirit is speaking because the Lord now uses what the devil meant for evil against me to help me exercise my spiritual senses in order to discern the good from the evil.

It helps to know how covenants are used by God, how the enemy also uses them and how we are to operate the covenant that we have with the Lord. You must apply the covenant of God in your life on a daily basis. Again, I say that if something gets so difficult and you do not see a way out, break bread. Get your communion elements and sit down and break bread with the Lord Jesus. He said that you are to remember Him as often as you break bread and drink the wine in His name.

> **"After the same manner also he took the cup, when he had supped, saying, This cup is the new testament in my blood: this do ye, as oft as ye drink it, in remembrance of me"** (1 Corinthians 11:25).

You should apply this in your life. I always ask the Lord to remember me as I remember Him during my communion taking. For instance John Chapter 5 is a very good scripture when you are in need of fruitfulness or harvest. You should use it to ask the Lord to remember you according to His Word and grant you a harvest or fruitfulness. God wants you to succeed and He wants you to bear fruit and for your fruit to abound. In other words, God does not want you to loose your harvest or fruitfulness.

There are some spirits that wait until a person has something in their hand; be it harvest, fruits or something valuable and the spirits will just come around and knock it off. That is why with some people, no matter how much you give them, they will always end up in the same place —broke! You can give them a million dollars, but in about six months to a year, they will be broke again and they cannot account for what they did with the money. The reason is because as soon as something valuable comes into their hands, the squandering spirit, the spirit of self indulgence, the spirit of recklessness and the spirit of stupidity just take over and it is just a question of time before they come back to their vagabond state. When they are back to being poor and destitute, all their common sense then comes back and they can now see how they could have handled their finances and the devil then begins to use their stupidity to harass them. He would begin to say to them, "You are stupid; look at what you did. Yea, you did this and you did that and oh, you really topped yourself when you did that one." Therefore, I say to you, learn to rely on the Lord and His covenant promises. Cry to Him to give you His wisdom and learn to apply His promises in your life.

When we know covenant we can begin to protect ourselves and walk in the way that God can manifest things for us faster. When you operate the covenant promises properly, the things that used to take years to manifest will begin to happen within a few months or weeks.

Divine Provision:

Divine provision is also promised to us in the New Covenant. It is our inheritance in Christ Jesus. Jesus told us in **John 16:23** that whatsoever we ask the Father in His name, He will give it to us.

This is like a blank check when you know what is yours in the New Covenant. During my prayer times, I like to remind the Lord of His Word in **Isaiah 65:24** that before I call, He will answer and that while I am yet speaking, He will hear.

One day, when I was praying, God the Father showed me in a vision of all my prayer petitions. He had a classroom board on His wall and He had written on it every prayer petition that I have ever made and also every prayer that I will ever pray in my life time. He looked at me and He looked at the prayers and petitions and He went to the board and He checked off knowledge. **According to Him, out of all my petitions, knowledge was what I needed the most and that is what He released to me that day. He said that I was yet too ignorant to walk in all the things that I was asking for. In His opinion, I needed knowledge and after that, I need wisdom (application of knowledge).** I do not believe that I am alone in lack of knowledge because a lot of Christians will read the Bible but will not apply its wisdom in their lives. This will greatly delay the manifestation of their blessings:

> **"Blessed be the God and Father of our Lord Jesus Christ, <u>who hath blessed us with all spiritual blessings in heavenly places in Christ</u>"** (Ephesians 1:3).

The truth is, if we do not have a practical application of the Word of God in our lives, we cannot succeed in life. Divine provision has been given to us but we need wisdom on how to appropriate it in our lives.

Divine Healing:

Divine healing is the portion of the believer. We are not a people without healing provisions. When we exercise our faith we can begin to walk in the healing anointing that is already given to us in Christ. Remember that **Isaiah 53:5** tells us that the Lord was wounded for our transgressions, He was bruised for our iniquity and that by His stripes we are healed?

> "**But he was wounded for our transgressions, he was bruised for our iniquities: the chastisement of our peace was upon him; <u>and with his stripes we are healed</u>.**"

Therefore we all need to rest in the knowledge that divine healing is already given to us in Christ Jesus. We also see it stated again in **1 Peter 2:22:**

> "**<u>Who his own self bare our sins in his own body</u> on the tree, that we, being dead to sins, should live unto righteousness: <u>by whose stripes ye WERE HEALED</u>.**"

The above scripture tells us that **we were healed**. It is in the past and so when you come to the Lord and you know you are having problems with your health, **remind Him in faith** of the covenant you have with Him. Then ask Him if there is an outstanding ungodly covenant with the devil in your life or in your family that is keeping the New Covenant in the blood of Jesus from being in operation in your life. Ask to know what it is because as a partaker of the New Covenant, divine health is yours.

Once He reveals the source of your affliction to you, you need to repent and once you have repented, begin to claim the covenant blessings of divine health. During my prayer times, I usually root up and pull down those things that I do not desire in my life. I will send the Word of God to destroy them and burn them up. But when I look back at the situation and it looks as if nothing has changed, I then turn to the Lord to help me understand what the hindrance is and I would remind Him that I did everything that He commanded me to do in His Word. Once He said to me, "Yes, you rooted up, you plucked up and you threw down and you destroyed but what did you plant?" I said, "Oh, nothing." He told me to go back and plant the things that I wanted to see happen. I learned from this that when I pluck up some things in my life, I need to replace them with good things. If not, the ground becomes fallow spiritually. The Lord Jesus told us that when we drive away an unclean spirit, we should not leave that place (house) empty and well garnished without sowing some good seeds in it because if we do not speak the right things into it, the evil spirit will see that it is empty and will ask other wicked spirits to help it stage a come back:

> " When **the unclean spirit is gone out of a man**, he walketh through dry places, seeking rest, and findeth none. *44* Then he saith, **I will return into my house from whence I came out; and when he is come, he findeth it empty, swept, and garnished.** *45* Then goeth he, and **taketh with himself seven other spirits more wicked than himself, and they enter in and dwell there: and the last state of that man is worse than the first…**" (Matthew 12: 43-45).

Therefore, when you root up, throw down and destroy, you must need build and plant righteousness because you have only done the first part by destroying the works of the enemy but you have to plant righteousness, peace and joy of the Holy Ghost in the field. Always remember to plant whatever you need; be it prosperity, success, health, etc., in the field. Use the Word of God correctly and if you are totally sold out to God, He too will be totally committed to you. He honors those that honor Him.

The Bond Slave Covenant:

If you look at me closely, you will notice that I only wear one earring on my right ear. I read the scripture in **Exodus 21:1-6** and it inspired me to want to be totally sold out to God as His bond slave. It says that if you have a slave and the slaves does not want to leave the master's house in the year of jubilee (7th year) when all slaves are set free but wants to stay with his master past his time of slavery, the master should bore a hole in the ear of the slave and the slave will belong to him forever. Although I am already His daughter, it became my heart's cry to belong to the Lord forever as His devoted servant –His slave! I know that some people do not like the idea of being a slave but with God, it is the best thing that can happen to you because you rest in Him while you just trust and obey His instructions.

> **"If thou buy an Hebrew servant, six years he shall serve: and in the seventh he shall go out free for nothing…5 <u>And if the servant shall plainly say</u>, <u>I love my master</u>, <u>my wife</u>, and <u>my children</u>; <u>I will not go out free</u>: 6 Then his master shall bring him unto the judges; <u>he shall also bring him to the door</u>, <u>or unto the door post</u>; and <u>his master shall bore his ear through with an aul</u>;** *(needle)* **and <u>he shall serve him for ever</u>."**

After reading this, I started crying out to the Him that I wanted to be totally sold out to Him; I wanted to be His bond slave. I kept at Him with the request and so one night, He woke me up and said, "Do you really want to be my bond slave?" I said, "Yes" and He said, "Do you know what a bond slave is? Do you know that a slave has no rights, no opinion on any matter and owns no property but only does as he is told?" I said, "Yes, that's what I want." He said, "Really?" and I said, "Yes." So, He pulled out a very long needle with a thread in it and He pierced my right ear. When I got to church the next day being Sunday, He said to me as we were worshiping, "Take off the earring on your left ear; I only pierced your right ear so that when you look in the mirror, you will always know whose bond slave you are." I took off the earring on my left ear and I have been His bond slave ever since.

As a result of this bond slave covenant with the Lord, whenever I insist on something to be done the way I like it or when I negotiate with the Lord for things to be done my way, He reminds me of our covenant of bond slave and I will look in the mirror and I say, "Ok, a slave does not have any opinion," and I will do as

He instructs me. You have to know how to walk with the Lord in order for your life not to be so strenuous and for things not to be so difficult for you because our God has not made walking with Him hard. It is just that so many things have been laid up against us for several generations and we have to set ourselves free from them.

I remember when I was a little girl and we would go to the farm and the person at the head of the group going through the forest had to use a sharp machete to cut away strong twines of ropes from the limbs of trees and a staff to disturb the ground in order not to step on the head of a snake when we were trying to make a pathway in the places that people have not gone through before or for a long time. You have to be very alert at such a time because you do not want to step on a snake and you do not want anything to jump on you from the tree tops. Everyone in the group is aware that we are trying to make a straight path and that we are essentially making a path for others to come behind us on.

For a lot of us, our Christian life is spent just making a pathway for others to come behind us in our families and amongst our friends. It might seem difficult and hard because you constantly have to plow and do warfare in order to reclaim the things that the devil had stolen from the generations before you. Be not discouraged because you are making a way for your children and your children's children. We are to leave a godly legacy for our children and for all the generations after us.

When you look at some ministers whose fathers or grandfathers were in ministry and have a godly legacy, you will see the godly heritage, prosperity and blessings that have been built up for them and they do not have the type of warfare in areas that most people without a Christian legacy do. We see this in terms of being able to get a ministry started because they inherited one, they know people in ministry through their parents and they have a name that can help them to become established financially. These people inherited something in their "destiny basket" that positioned them for blessings, prosperity and success. For somebody like me that is from Africa, it was nothing but curses from ancestral practices of witchcraft, divination, sorcery, necromancy, etc., so God essentially had to pour the vile of curses out of my life and make sure that it was empty and He had to remove their negative effects from my life. He also had to help me to build a "destiny basket of blessings" and a godly heritage so that I could have a chance of having significance and building something of value in life and for the generations after me. Therefore, I purposed to appropriate for myself, all the benefits that are in the covenants that we have with God through Christ and Abraham.

I have told you about things that are God's duties to perform, the things that are already given to us and I stated that one of those things is divine healing. We now know that God has ordained us to be fruitful and that God has already blessed us with all spiritual blessings. I remember one day when I was being taught the Bible and the scripture that God has already blessed us with all spiritual blessings in heavenly places and the pastor said to me, **"What you do is imagine that you are standing in a vast field and there are so many blessings just floating around above you and your job is to just reach out and pluck; yes, just reach out and pluck."** I understood it to mean that God has already done for us what we want —all spiritual blessings are given to me already. I do not have to ask God for blessings but ask Him for the manifestation of the blessings in my life!

This is why Jesus said that when we pray, we should ask that God's will be done on earth as it has already been done in heaven. Therefore, if there is a particular blessing that is not manifested in your life, then you say, "Ok Lord, this blessing is given to me by the virtue of the covenant that I have with You and I need to see the manifestation of it in my life. You do not speak to God rudely, you do not give Him an ultimatum but you ask Him in reverence and in humility. Always remember that God does not owe anyone of us anything and that He willingly humbled Himself to deal with us through a covenant. Also, know that God works in cooperation with you. He will not do everything for you while you do nothing. All His promises are conditional. There are conditions that you must meet in order to receive what you ask for. His way is usually "If you do…, then I will bless you with…"

Do not act as a woman we met during a ministry trip did concerning her petitions to God. She is a very good and kind hearted woman and she is not a poor woman either. She just did not understand God's principles about giving. She loves to give finances to ministries because it is her passion. As a result, she had in her church a huge table with lots and lots of papers. She told me that they were records of her financial gifts and seeds to people and to other ministries. She had been praying and believing for a breakthrough from the Lord and many other ministers have gone over to pray with her and she still has not seen any breakthrough. Therefore, she got together with a minister from out of town who had "a new perspective on how to get a breakthrough" and according to her, the minister presented her case concerning her petitions and records of giving in heaven. The minister had the case tried in heaven and she won! I said to her, "He had you and God tried in a case in heaven and you won? Who did he say was the looser in the case?" I never got the answer as to who lost. I know that she is a good woman of God who has been given the wrong information on how to get a breakthrough by the visiting minister. Therefore, I say to you, beware of wrong teaching.

Always remember that it is not a case of you and God in a trial and do not get legalistic. God is not on trial because you are only reminding Him about His promises. If there is a problem with your prayers not being answered, always know that the fault is not on God's side but yours. It was so funny because when this woman called me aside to put in her prayer request, I was not aware that a visiting minister had "tried her case in heaven and that she had won" but the Lord said to me, "Tell her that I am not deaf. Tell her that I heard her but I will not give her what she is asking for because she is not a good steward." The Lord began to show me that most of her giving has not been at the leading of the Holy Spirit. She has actually been playing God in some people's lives. God's Word to her was to cut it out. I gave her the Word of the Lord and told her to make changes concerning her giving and to rely on the leading of the Holy Spirit.

God hears everything and God knows everything so when you do not see an answer to your prayers, stop and ask Him the nature of agreement or covenant that you are dealing with that seeks to hinder answers to your prayers. The reason as I stated before is because when there is a covenant in place, even if someone prays for you, you might get a release for one or two days and then the condition will come right back because the devil will claim his covenant right to afflict you in that area. He will fight for the legal right that he has to come back and he will come back until you or someone decides that enough is enough and drives him away by first repenting and then renouncing the covenant with him.

Our Duties:

As I stated before, there are things God will not do for us because He expects us to do them in the name of Jesus. The Lord Jesus gave us His delegated power to do certain things. For example, it is our duty to pray, to preach the Gospel, to heal the sick, to cast out devils, to raise the dead and to cleanse the lepers. We see this in the following scriptures.

> "**Call unto me, and I will answer thee, and shew thee great and mighty things, which thou knowest not**" (Jeremiah 33:3).

It is our duty to call upon God (pray) so that He will come into our situations. He gave the earth to the children of men and we are to call when we need Him. We are the ones sent to preach.

> "**And as ye go, preach, saying, The kingdom of heaven is at hand. 8 Heal the sick, cleanse the lepers, raise the dead, cast out devils: freely ye have received, freely give**" (Matthew 10:7-8).

We cannot ask God to do these things because He is expecting us to do them in the name of Jesus. The Lord once told me to rebuke an intercessor who was praying that God should open the eyes of the unbeliever as they go by the church sign so that they can come into the church and get saved. In response, the Lord told me to rebuke her for praying such a prayer and to remind her that He commanded us to go out and preach the Gospel and not wait for the unbelievers to come to us.

> "Then he called his twelve disciples together, **and gave them power and authority over all devils**, **and to cure diseases**. *2* And he sent them to preach the kingdom of God, and to heal the sick" (Luke 9:12).

> "And into whatsoever city ye enter, and they receive you, eat such things as are set before you: *9* And **heal the sick that are therein**, and **say unto them, The kingdom of God is come nigh unto you**" (Luke 10:8-9).

When we truly understand our duties and God's duties concerning our covenant with Him, it will affect **our worship**, **prayers**, **our words, our actions and our associations**. We all need to examine ourselves in order to see if the reason we have not been experiencing God's covenant blessings, deliverance and healing is because we are misapplying His covenant. Are we expecting Him to do the things that He already gave us His delegated authority and power to do? As I sated before, the Bible tells us who we are in Christ and I outlined some scriptures earlier in the previous chapter that help us to see that. Below are some more scriptures that tell us who we are:

1. **A chosen generation:** "But ye are a **chosen generation**, a royal priesthood, an holy nation, a peculiar people; that ye should shew forth the praises of him who hath called you out of darkness into his marvelous light"(I Peter 2:9).

2. **Heirs of God and joint-heirs with Christ:** "And if children, then heirs; **heirs of God**, and **joint-heirs with Christ**; if so be that we suffer **with** him, that we may be also glorified together" (Romans 8:17).

3. **We are raised up together with Christ:** "And hath **raised**

us up together, and made us sit together in heavenly places in Christ Jesus" (Ephesians 2:6).

4. **We reign in life by Jesus Christ:** "Much more they which receive abundance of grace and of the gift of righteousness **shall reign in life by one, Jesus Christ**." We are to rule and reign with Christ" (Romans 5:17).

5. **We are to occupy till He comes:** We are to **"occupy till He comes."** (Luke 19:13).

6. **We are the epistles of Christ written by the Holy Spirit:** "Forasmuch as ye are manifestly **declared to be the epistle of Christ** ministered by us, written not with ink, but with the Spirit of the Living God; not in tables of stone, but in fleshy tables of the heart" (II Corinthians 3:3).

7. **We are ambassadors for Christ:** "Now then **we are ambassadors** for Christ, as though God did beseech you by us: we pray you in Christ's stead, be ye reconciled to God" (II Corinthians 5:20).

8. **We are the salt of the earth:** "Ye are **the salt of the earth**: but if **the salt** have lost his savour, wherewith shall it be salted? It is thenceforth good for nothing, but to be cast out, and to be trodden under foot of men" (Matthew 5:13).

9. **We are the light of the world:** "Ye are **the light of the world**. A city that is set on an hill cannot be hid" (Matthew 5:14).

10. **We stand before God as holy, unblameable and unreproveable:** "In the body of his flesh through death, **to present you holy and unblameable and unreproveable in his sight**" (Colossians 1:22).

Although, we are all these things in Christ, we can still fall short of what God has for us if we operate His covenants incorrectly or if we do not understand how He uses covenants.

A Look at How God Uses Covenant:

We are now going to take a look at some scriptures in order to see how God operates covenants through His Son Jesus Christ. We will also see the reaction of the Lord Jesus when people operated covenants incorrectly with Him. We have to learn how God operates His covenants.

The Pharisees and the Lord Over the Sabbath Law

The Bible tells us that God gave the children of Israel a law to rest on the Sabbath day. According to God, they shall work six (6) days but must rest on the seventh (7th) day and anyone who violates this law was to be put to death. We see this in **Exodus 31:14-15**:

> **"Observe the Sabbath, because it is holy to you. Anyone who desecrates it must be put to death; whoever does any work on that day must be cut off from his people. *15* For six days, work is to be done, but the seventh day is a Sabbath of rest, holy to the Lord. Whoever does any work on the Sabbath day must be put to death."**

This was the law (the Old Covenant) that was in Israel until the arrival of the Lord Jesus. As we can see, it is very specific about what must be done to anyone who violates the law of the Sabbath. When the Lord showed up on the scene, He did not play by the law of the Sabbath. He healed the sick on the Sabbath, cast out devils on the Sabbath, opened the blind eyes on the Sabbath and He told a man whom He had healed on the Sabbath to pick up His bed and go home! As a result, the Pharisees (the leaders) were "convinced" that He was not from God and that He was not using the power of God because He did not operate in the Old Covenant.

The friction between the Lord and the Jewish leaders is best illustrated by the scripture in **John Chapter 9** when the Lord healed a man that was blind from birth on the Sabbath. When the Pharisees heard about it, they began to question the man because they did not believe that the Lord performed the miracle besides, He did it on the Sabbath which to them was a clear sign that the Lord was not from God.

> **"They brought to the Pharisees him that aforetime was blind.** *14* <u>**And it was the sabbath day when Jesus made the clay, and opened his eyes**</u>**.** *15* **Then again the Pharisees also asked him how he had received his sight. He said unto them,** <u>**He put clay upon mine eyes**</u> *(the Lord worked on the Sabbath),* **and I washed, and do see.** *16* **Therefore said some of the Pharisees,** <u>**This man is not of God, because he keepeth not the sabbath day**</u>**. Others said, How can a man that is a sinner do such miracles?"** (John 9:13-16).

But what they did not know was that the Lord Jesus is the **Lord of the Sabbath** and therefore was not bound by the law of the Sabbath. He came full of GRACE and TRUTH to save them rather than let the LAW continue to condemn them to death. He tried to explain this to them by saying to them:

> **"For the Son of man is Lord even of the sabbath day"** (Matthew 12:8).

The Pharisees were so closed minded that they refused to listen to the Lord. He again said to them that God made the Sabbath for man and not man for the Sabbath:

> **"And he said unto them,** <u>**The sabbath was made for man, and not man for the sabbath**</u>**"** (Matthew 2:27).

He was not bound by the law of Sabbath because God the Father is not bound by the law of the Sabbath. He told them in **John 5:16-17** that He works on the Sabbath because His Father (God) works on the Sabbath!

> "And therefore did <u>the Jews persecute Jesus, and sought to slay him, because he had done these things on the sabbath day.</u> *17* <u>But Jesus answered them, My Father worketh hitherto, and I work</u>."

What the Jewish leaders did not understand was that the Lord was actually sent to deliver them from the death sentence of the law. He was offering them a way out of the condemnation that they were in under the LAW, but they could not see the New Covenant of love and mercy that He was offering them. This is why **John 1:17** tells us that:

> "For the <u>law was given by Moses</u>, but <u>grace and truth came by Jesus Christ</u>."

The Lord was operating the New Covenant of grace while the Pharisees were operating the Old Covenant of death. Therefore, there was always friction between them because the Pharisees were not willing to receive God's grace that came through the Lord Jesus Christ.

The Syro-Phoenician Woman

I know a lot of people have heard or read this story about the Syro-Phoenician woman or the Canaanite woman. This woman had a daughter that was tormented by demons so she came to Jesus as reported in **Matthew 15:21-28**. We will see from this scripture how this woman incorrectly operates a covenant and we will see how the Lord responded.

> "Then Jesus went thence, and departed into the coasts of Tyre and Sidon. *22* And, <u>behold, a woman of Canaan came out of the same coasts</u>, and cried unto him, saying, <u>Have mercy on me, O Lord, thou</u>

Son of David; my daughter is grievously vexed with a devil. *23* **But he answered her not a word**. And his disciples came and besought him, saying, Send her away; for she crieth after us. *24* **But he answered and said, I am not sent but unto the lost sheep of the house of Israel.** *25* **Then came she and worshipped him, saying, Lord, help me.** *26* But he answered and said, **It is not meet to take the children's bread, and to cast it to dogs.** *27* And she said, Truth, Lord: yet the dogs eat of the crumbs which fall from their masters' table. *28* Then Jesus answered and said unto her, O woman, great is thy faith: be it unto thee even as thou wilt. And her daughter was made whole from that very hour."

This woman is from Canaan and the Canaanites are not partaker of the Abrahamic Covenant that the Lord Jesus was sent by God the Father to fulfill. She cried unto the Lord saying, **"Have mercy on me O Lord, thou Son of David."** What she just did was invoked a covenant that she has no right to benefit from and **the Lord recognizes that she is not aware of what she just did and as a result, He goes silent!** Jesus is the Son of David and David is from the lineage of Abraham and the Apostle Paul tells us that Jesus is the Seed of Abraham to whom all the promises in Abraham pertains —**"Now to Abraham and his seed were the promises made. He saith not, And to seeds, as of many; but as of one, And to thy seed, which is Christ"** (Galatians 3:16). As I have said several times already, we the believers have a right to the benefits of the **Abrahamic Covenant** only because we are in Christ.

This woman invokes the **Abrahamic Covenant by appealing to the Lord as the Son of David and this creates a problem that she is not aware of.** God cut His covenant with Abraham and his seed and the Canaanite do not have a right to the covenant. The Canaanites are not descendants of Abraham. If you are not aware of how God operates covenant you will wonder; what is wrong with Jesus? Does He not have compassion on a woman with a sick daughter? The Bible says that **He answered her not a word** because she is not aware that she had just put Him in a bind. He knows she had just invoked the wrong covenant as a Canaanite person; she went where she was not supposed to go and He cannot move on her behalf under the **Abrahamic Covenant**.

Remember when He told the disciples to go heal the sick and cast out devils that He told them to do it in Judea but not to go to Samaria? He said go not into Samaria because **God the Father sent Him to the Jews only:**

> **"These twelve Jesus sent forth, and commanded them, saying, Go not into the way of the Gentiles, and into any city of the Samaritans enter ye not: 6 But go rather to the lost sheep of the house of Israel"** (Matthew 10:5-6).

It was not until the Jews rejected Him that salvation was made available to "whosoever will." Therefore, this woman invoked a covenant that she has no right to invoke and Jesus could not respond under the covenant, so He answered her not a word!

His disciples had no idea what was going on with the Lord concerning this woman so they decided He should send her away —**"And his disciples came and besought him, saying, Send her away; for she crieth after us."** The Lord then decided to let the woman know what was wrong with her request: **"But he answered and said, I am not sent but unto the lost sheep of the house of Israel."** In other words, I am only sent to those who have a covenant with the Living God through Abraham. It was not that Jesus did not love her but He would be transgressing the instructions from heaven if He operated under the Abrahamic Covenant for a non-Jew.

This woman needed an answer so even though she is not a Jew, she knew enough that Jesus was also the LORD OF ALL so **"she came and worshipped him, saying, 'Lord, help me.'"** She changed the situation by moving away from the Son of David covenant request into the Lordship of Jesus Christ. Jesus is Lord of both the Jews and the Gentiles because He is Lord of all. The Lord is still trying to make her understand about covenant so He says to her; "**It is not meet to take the children's bread** *(God's provision for the Jews)***, and to cast it to dogs.**" The woman in turn agrees that she does not have a right to the Abrahamic Covenant but Jesus is her **Lord and master so she needs His crumbs** —"**And she said, Truth, Lord: yet the dogs eat of** <u>**the crumbs which fall from their masters' table**</u>**.** She acknowledged to the Lord that yes, she is not a partaker of this covenant but You are my Lord and You are my Master and as a result of moving away from the Abrahamic Covenant, Jesus' hands were no longer tied from helping her by the Abrahamic Covenant so He was elated and screamed, "**O woman, great is thy faith: be it unto thee even as thou wilt.**" So, you see how the covenant that she invoked (the Son of David) could have kept her from getting something from the Lord? Therefore, we must know how to use covenant properly. She received a breakthrough for her daughter when she moved into the Lordship of the Lord.

Without knowing what she was doing, she was able to invoke the right covenant —the New Covenant that the Lord came to establish with whosoever will believe in Him. She went into the New Covenant where Jesus is Lord of all and under which He can operate on behalf of the Gentiles. She essentially became a believer in the Lord Jesus Christ and it is one reason that the Lord was just so pleased with her. She got more than she asked for —all the benefits of the New Covenant. This is why we need to know how to use covenants when we pray.

I remember how on one occasion the Lord rebuked me during my prayer time. This was not even a wrongful use of covenant issue but wrongful use of the relationship of the Godhead. I was saying some things to the Lord Jesus in prayer and He immediately interjected and rebuked me. While praising Him, I had said to Him without paying attention to what I said, "You are above all and none is greater than You are…" and He said, "Stop right there; I taught you better than that. Did I not tell you that my Father is greater than I? Cut it out!" What I learned from it, is that we all have to be careful not to place the Lord Jesus above the Father in our zeal or in our love for Jesus because if we do, we would be misrepresenting the relationship of the Godhead. **It is really all about the Father because the Bible tells us that the Lord Himself is going to deliver the church to the Father and place Himself under the Father so that God can "be all in all."**

> "Then cometh the end, <u>when he *(Jesus)* shall have delivered up the kingdom to God, even the Father</u>; when he shall have put down all rule and all authority and power. *25* For he must reign, till he hath put all enemies under his feet…*28* <u>And when all things shall be subdued unto him, then shall the Son also himself be subject unto him that put all things under him, that God may be all in all</u>" (1 Corinthians 15:24-28).

We have to make sure that some of the things that we say about Jesus line up with what He taught us about the Father, Himself and the Holy Spirit. We also have to make sure that we are operating His covenant correctly because each time someone invokes the wrong covenant, He will become silent.

The Woman Caught in Adultery

This account of events again shows what happens when people come to the Lord and they invoke the wrong covenant. We are going to take a look at this in **John 8:1-12**; I call this LAW vs. GRACE. The Lord was in the middle of a teaching in the temple when the Scribes, the Pharisees and their supporters disrupted His teaching session by dragging to Him a woman who was caught in the very act of adultery. They wanted to trap the Lord and to show publicly that He was not an observer of the Law of Moses.

> "**Jesus went unto the mount of Olives.** *2* **And early in the morning <u>he came again into the temple, and</u>**

> **all the people came unto him; and he sat down, and taught them.** *3* And the scribes and Pharisees **brought unto him a woman taken in adultery; and when they had set her in the midst,** *4* They say unto him, **Master, this woman was taken in adultery, in the very act.** *5* **Now Moses in the law commanded us, that such should be stoned: but what sayest thou?** *6* This they said, tempting him, that they might have to accuse him. **But Jesus stooped down, and with his finger wrote on the ground, as though he heard them not** *(the Lord is again silent because they are trying to operate the wrong covenant with Him).* *7* **So when they continued asking him**, he lifted up himself, and said unto them, **He that is without sin among you, let him first cast a stone at her.** *8* **And again he stooped down, and wrote on the ground** *(He knows that they are all under condemnation as sinners by the law of Moses).* *9* **And they which heard it, being convicted by their own conscience, went out one by one, beginning at the eldest, even unto the last:** *(they all got condemned by the law and left shamefully)* **and Jesus was left alone, and the woman standing in the midst.** *10* When Jesus had lifted up himself, and saw none but the woman, he said unto her, Woman, where are those thine accusers? hath no man condemned thee? *11* She said, No man, Lord. **And Jesus said unto her, Neither do I condemn thee: go, and sin no more** *(this is Grace).* *12* Then spake Jesus again unto them, saying, I am the light of the world: he that followeth me shall not walk in darkness, but shall have the light of life."

What the Jewish leaders failed or refused to accept was that God sent them His mercy through His Son Jesus but they were blinded by their traditions and could not see it. They hated Jesus because they had their own agenda and they never really bothered to find out who Jesus really was. Had they investigated His birth, they would have seen that He was from the house of David but because He grew up in Nazareth, they ruled Him off. They did not believe that anything good can come out of Nazareth; especially a prophet. The Lord saw their ignorance so **He stooped down and with His finger wrote on the ground and acted as though He did not hear them.**

They were invoking the Old Covenant (the Law) and He was offering them the New Covenant (grace and mercy). Remember that the Lord also went silent when the Syro-Phoenician woman invoked the wrong covenant with Him. **From these two incidents involving the wrongful use of covenant, you can see that the Lord has a pattern of becoming silent when someone invokes a wrong covenant with Him;** He stops speaking and becomes silent; in this case, He wrote on the ground. The last time **the finger of God wrote something on the wall was in Daniel 5:24-28** to Belshazzar (Nebuchadnezzar's son) and it was judgment. See it below:

> "Then was the <u>part of the hand sent from him; and this writing was written</u>. *25* And this is the writing that was written, **MENE, MENE, TEKEL, UPHARSIN.** *26* This is the interpretation of the thing: MENE; God hath numbered thy kingdom, and finished it. *27* TEKEL; <u>Thou art weighed in the balances, and art found wanting.</u> *28* **PERES;** <u>**Thy kingdom is divided, and given to the Medes and Persians**</u> *(God's judgment).*

We can safely deduce that in the case of the lady caught in adultery, the Lord had written a judgment on the sand for anyone who will be the first person to cast a stone at her. If anyone had cast a stone at the woman, that person would have received that judgment as an example to the rest of the people. When God's finger writes, it is something serious.

We see from this incident the clash of LAW vs. GRACE. The Old Covenant called for the woman's death by stoning but the New Covenant granted her grace and mercy. **The Old Covenant has room only for judgment, condemnation and death but the**

New Covenant has room for grace and it has room for mercy. Therefore, when we are invoking covenant, we have to know even in our prayers to the Lord the terms of the covenants that we are invoking. If you are partaking of the New Covenant, do not also invoke the Old Covenant that the Lord nailed to His Cross. I say this because many of us still try to relate to God as though we are still under the Old Covenant but the Word of God tells us in **Romans 6:14** that we are not under the law but under grace. The law was never made for the Gentiles but for the Jews only:

> **"For sin shall not have dominion over you: <u>for ye are not under the law, but under grace</u>."**

We also read in **Colossians 2:14** that Christ has blotted out the ordinances of the law and nailed them to the cross because we could not keep them:

> **"Blotting out the handwriting of ordinances** *(the Law)* **that was against us, which was contrary to us, and took it out of the way, nailing it to his cross."**

We are also to operate in grace and mercy and not judgment, condemnation and death when dealing with other people. We send the Word of God to destroy the devil, his evil spirits and their evil works and not people's lives because God wants people saved. The Lord died so that men and women can be saved.

As I just showed you above, the Bible tells us **that Jesus has nailed the Old Covenant (the Law) to His Cross.** Therefore, you have to check your prayers; check what you say to the Lord to make sure that you are in the place that you are supposed to be in terms of covenant relationship. If you do not, you will be praying prayers that God cannot answer under the New Covenant of grace and you will wonder why He has not moved on your behalf. This is why I like the *"cleansing prayers"* in my prayer book titled, ***Effective Prayers for Various Situations, Vol. 1*** because if you have prayed without wisdom or others have spoken or prayed about you contrary to God's will, then you need divine assistance in order to purge the prayers. You need to pluck up and destroy such prayers and words and you need to replace them with God's blessings for you. You want them plucked up so that His will can come to pass in the area of your life that has been affected. Some of us are like little rockets and we just decree things according to our emotions without checking to see if we are keeping the terms of the covenant that we have with God. Praying effectively therefore requires that we all know the terms of the New Covenant and that we learn to keep and use the terms when we pray and make supplications unto the Lord.

How to Put God in Remembrance of His Covenant:

The Lord Jesus came to help us understand the ways of God and according to **Hebrews 1:1-3,** He is the express image of God the Father. The Lord showed us that God cares about us and loves us. He showed us that God answers when we call unto Him and He wants to speak to us:

> "**<u>God</u>, who at sundry times and in divers manners spake in time past unto the fathers by the prophets, 2 Hath in <u>these last days spoken unto us by his Son</u>, <u>whom he hath appointed heir of all things</u>, by whom also he made the worlds; 3 <u>Who being the brightness of his glory, and the express image of his person</u>, and upholding all things by the word of his power...**"

In other words, the Lord came to help us put a face to God and He came with grace, truth and mercy for all who will receive Him. If you wanted to see what God looked like physically, all you had to do is take a look at Jesus. Even today, if you want to see God's perspective on an issue, look at what Jesus had to say about it. You do not have to go any further seeking what God the Father would say because Jesus completely expressed the Father.

If we do not know what we are doing, we can be summoning God or invoking Him under a covenant where He cannot move on our behalf. You do not want to ask for something and have God go silent until you get corrected and then come back again to ask properly. Some people I know have been waiting for something for twenty years and God has probably said something to them or they are using a scripture that is not the scripture for us today, then they wonder why God does not move. They can waste many years waiting for answers and not get one until someone corrects them about their request.

You have to know who you are and you have to know what God has done for you so that when you go to invoke this covenant with Him, you will invoke it properly. As I stated before, **I usually invoke the New Covenant by breaking bread because it is the one thing that the Lord Jesus told us to do when He said, "Do this in remembrance of me."** I get the elements (bread and wine); I know that some people are very spiritual so they do not use wine. I use real wine because Jesus never drank grape juice; He drank real wine. I say, Lord, I am doing this in obedience to Your Word and according to the covenant that You established with Your blood. I am doing it in remembrance of You and I need You to also remember me and to see where I am right now; remember what my situation is right now and arise on my behalf and manifest Your salvation for me in this area. When you do that in faith, you will move the hand of God on your behalf like you will not believe.

As I stated before, when I go to Him and humbly and politely state my request to Him using the terms of the covenant, He will tell me, "You've made your point." If it is something like a huge request like the last one I made on my last birthday and I was enraged because I did not see the answer, I will then restate the terms of the covenant to Him. In this particular case, He gave me a vision of what I asked for and how it was too small in His eyes and what He has already done for me concerning my request. When I saw it, I was amazed because it was ten times more than what I had asked for and as a result, I began to praise Him and I began to thank

Him for His faithfulness in keeping covenants. I am in a season of great expectation because what has been done for me is awesome and it is way more than what I asked for. This is why I say that you have to know how to operate the New Covenant properly in order for you to begin to walk in the covenant blessings.

Note: *Pray the prayer of repentance (below) for areas where you have invoked the wrong covenant that has put you in a place where you cannot receive what the Lord has for you. You do not want the Lord to become silent and unable to move on your behalf because you are operating the Old Covenant. Let the Abrahamic Covenant and the New Covenant be the only covenants that govern the prayers and petitions that you place before the Lord.*

This might sound simple but it will transform your prayer life and affect how quickly you receive answers to your prayers. If you do not know what you are doing when it comes to covenants, you will find yourself praying without getting answers. I also encourage the reader to go and study the scriptures concerning the life of Elisha. Elisha was someone who walked with the Lord and he was aware of what was going on around him because he heard clearly from the Lord and was very much aware of who God made and called him to be according to the Old Covenant. Elisha knew things about God, circumstances, people, places and how his day was going to be on a daily basis. Therefore, he was genuinely shocked that God did not tell him that the Shunamite woman's son was going to die or that he was dead! He was amazed that something that serious was going to happen and God did not tell him.

He relied solely on the Lord and operated according to the authority and power that the Lord gave him. He never doubted the power of God that operated in him and through him. He was not like some of us who have the Lord's command and delegated authority to go and heal the sick, cast out devils, raise the dead, etc., in the name of Jesus but who turn around and ask the Lord to do it instead of carrying out the command in boldness and in faith. This is the kind of relationship that each one of us should have with the Lord;

where you know what is happening around you and you are not shocked by the things that happen around you. The Bible asks in **Isaiah 42:19**, "Who is the servant of the Lord that is blind?" You must have revelation about your life, about what you are dealing with and about what is going on around you so that you will know how to pray, what to decree or what to do. When you have revelation of what is going on around you and you know how to operate covenant properly, you will have a profound impact spiritually and physically when you speak. I have just showed you from scriptures that God becomes silent when you are invoking the wrong covenant. Therefore, you need to speak correctly and effectively.

Prayer to Renounce Wrong Covenants

"Father, in the name of the Lord Jesus I come before You and I thank You Lord that You are the God who keeps covenants even when we fail to keep them. Lord God, I thank You that You are our Father and also our teacher. I come as a student and I come as Your child and I ask Father, in the name of the Lord Jesus Christ that You forgive me of all the times that I invoked the wrong covenant in my petitions to You; even my wrongful use of covenants that made You to become silent in releasing answers to me.

"Father, I declare that I am no longer partaking of the Old Covenant ignorantly and that I am now only partaking of the New Covenant. Therefore, in the name of Jesus, I am asking for forgiveness and I am asking that You let my prayers, my petitions, my supplications, my decrees and my declarations be governed only by the New Covenant that You established with the blood of Jesus. Lord God, I acknowledge that You have given me a better covenant with better promises and Father, I thank You for it. Forgive me for the times that I had operated

the Old Covenant in my life and I also forgive those who taught me to hold on to the Old Covenant that has held me bound in religion instead of a loving relationship with You.

"I choose to operate the New Covenant and I ask that You cleanse me with the blood of Jesus from my wrongful use of covenants. I choose to learn from the teaching of the Apostle Paul in the book of Galatians not to abandon grace for the law. I choose to receive Your grace and walk in it and not try to earn my own righteousness through works. I know that I was saved by Your grace, I am kept by Your grace, I am healed by Your grace and provided for by Your grace. I choose to walk accordingly from now on.

"Father, I come out of agreement with those who had taught me to walk according to the Covenant that You are not operating in my life. I renounce all religious doctrines of bondage that are rooted in wrong teachings about the Old Covenant in the name of Jesus; I decree that as a new creation in Christ Jesus, I am governed by the New Covenant that is in the blood of Jesus. I renounce every decree, every declaration and every prayer that I had prayed erroneously using the wrong covenant. Father, forgive me and let those decrees be nullified now by the blood of Jesus; let them be replaced by the New Covenant that is in the blood of Jesus.

"I repent for going back to observing the Sabbath according to the Old Covenant. I know now that the Lord Jesus is "the Lord of the Sabbath" and that He is my Sabbath rest. Lord, I thank you for the divine enablement; even the Holy Spirit that the Lord Jesus said shall teach me all things and bring all things to my remembrance. Lord Holy Spirit, I ask

right now that You teach me how to operate the New Covenant in God's way so that I will no longer hinder the answers to my prayers and so that I can begin to walk in covenant blessings all the days of my life.

"Father, I thank You for Your grace that is already in me and I now stir up Your gifts within me by an act of my will and by faith in the name of Jesus. Help me to go forth in Your knowledge and the application of Your wisdom in the name of Jesus."

Note: *Some Christians actually go back to observing some aspects of the Law because of wrong teachings. If you are one of such people, repent for going back to the Law after the Lord died and paid for you to be set free from it. You must remember that the Law was not made for the Gentiles but for the Jews. In the New Covenant, the commandments are written in the hearts of whosoever will believe and this includes both the Jews and the Gentiles. Keeping the Law cannot make one righteous but the blood of Jesus can, so choose the correct covenant.*

Chapter 3

Overcoming the Devil's Legalities & Technicalities

According to **Proverbs 6:1-2** it matters who you make a covenant with:

> "**My son, if thou be surety for thy friend, <u>if thou hast stricken thy hand with a stranger</u>** *(made a covenant with a stranger),* **2 <u>Thou art snared with the words of thy mouth, thou art taken with the words of thy mouth</u>.**"

Your words and your actions can either bring you a blessing or a curse and they can also bring you into the devil's bondage forever. Also, the words and actions of the generations before you can greatly impact your life positively or negatively. Therefore, you need to read this chapter very carefully.

One of the things that I have been trying to do in this book is lay a solid foundation for you because I believe the saying that, **"when you teach a man to fish, you will feed him for a lifetime whereas if you give a man a fish, you only feed him for a day."** Therefore, in the previous chapters, I went to the root of one of the areas that keeps us from being effective in the kingdom of God and by this I mean, those areas in which we have covenants with the devil. I talked about the power of covenants and about how God uses covenants because it is not enough for you to know what you are not supposed to do but you must know what you are supposed to do.

We saw in the scriptures that whenever someone invoked a covenant that they have no legal right to invoke, Jesus went silent. We saw it in the case of the Canaanite woman who did not have a legal right to the benefits or the blessings that are in the Abrahamic

Covenant but she invoked it in ignorance and the Lord said nothing to her but kept silent to the point that the disciples said, well, He does not want to talk to her. They then advised the Lord to send her away. Then, by divine grace she moved out of the Abrahamic Covenant and into another type of covenant, the Lordship of Jesus Christ! She appealed to His Lordship, she worshiped Him and said, "Lord help me" and because He is Lord of all, He was able to help her but under the Abrahamic Covenant, He told her that He was only sent to the "lost sheep of the house of Israel."

You also saw when the Jews disrupted the Lord's teaching session by dragging in a woman that they caught in the very act of adultery. They said to Him, we caught this woman in adultery; in the very act and the Old Covenant which is the law said that we should stone such to death. What do you say? Again, just like in the case of the Canaanite woman, the Lord became silent and He began to write on the ground and when He eventually raised up His head, He said to them, the one person among you who has no sin, let that person be the first person to cast a stone at her. No one could cast the first stone because the very law that they were quoting also condemned every single one of them as a sinner! They were not willing to receive the grace and mercy that came by the Lord Jesus Christ. Under the Old Covenant, she was guilty but under the New Covenant which contains the grace and mercy of God through Christ, she was given a pardon and a total forgiveness.

Now I am going to talk about how the devil uses covenants. The devil is legalistic and if you arm him against you ignorantly, he will use whatever you armed him with against you. Because the heathens were directly under the devil's control and they worshipped him ignorantly, God told the children of Israel not to make any covenants with them when they got to the land of Canaan. God knew the power of covenants and the ways of the devil so He did not want the children of Israel to be ensnared by the devil through a covenant with the heathens around them. We see this is **Exodus 34:12**:

"Take heed to thyself, <u>lest thou make a covenant</u>

with the inhabitants of the land whither thou goest, **lest it be for a snare in the midst of thee…"**

The plan of the devil is to get you into a covenant agreement with him so that he can keep God from moving on your behalf and so that he can operate freely in your life. He does not care how he gets you into an agreement with him as long as you have an agreement with him. We learned from **Amos 3:3** that two have to be in agreement in order to walk together:

"Can two walk together, except they be agreed?"

It is a spiritual law that two must be in agreement for something to happen on earth. Therefore, God wants your agreement and the devil also wants your agreement. When God wants to move on planet earth, He looks for a person to agree with Him. Nothing is established on earth if a man or a woman is not in agreement. As a result, the devil wants your agreement any which way he can. He is always ready to make your ungodly ways, actions and words a permanent agreement with him. A case in point was a pregnant lady in one of the places where I had worked briefly. She heard that some old lady had died in her sleep and the first thing out of her mouth was, "Oh God, that is how I want to go." As soon as she said it, I saw the spirit of death descend upon her cubical and when I got up to look at her, I saw that she was about seven months pregnant. Before this incident, I had seen a vision in which I was being sent to an office to rescue somebody that death was so sure that he could claim with ease but I did not see the face of the person. However, I saw that the person's office had boxes packed and stacked in front of it.

I had only been in this office for about two weeks and as I was thinking about what to do because the lady's words invited the spirit of death against her, I noticed the stacked boxes in front of her cubical and they were the same boxes that I had seen in the vision. I then realized that the pregnant lady was the person that I was sent to rescue in that office. I had to be careful because it was a workplace so I prayed and I asked the Lord for wisdom on how to talk to the lady. He gave me the wisdom to invite her out to lunch so, I invited her to lunch and I made it my treat. During lunch, I told her that I was a born again Christian and I began to talk to her about the power of our confessions and the power of our words. It was clear to me after talking with her for a while that she was not in church but I gently let her know that I had overheard her confession concerning death. I was careful not scare her by telling her my vision but instead, I talked to her about the implication of her words. I said it might sound like a good thing to want to die in your sleep but did you realize that you are pregnant and will soon be in the delivery ward in a hospital? I said, suppose you go under anesthesia, would you want to wake up? She said yes. I told her that she might want to cancel her confession because it was a blanket statement that the devil can use any day he wants. I told her that she did not want the devil to come and collect on her words before she was ready and she was amazed that the devil could do that and so she cancelled her words. If the Lord had not sent me to that office, the devil would have taken out that lady during her delivery. As a matter of fact, he was so sure that he already had the soul but God proved him otherwise.

Not quite three days later the Lord moved me from that office to another because it was in a season that He told me that He and I were going on a journey to different places of work. According to Him, He wanted to show me the types of principalities and powers that "My children deal with in the workplace." He told me to sign up in a temporary agency and I did but I felt like I was being treated like the Prophet Isaiah except that I was not told to go naked. The Lord took me to different work environments and taught me about how the devil operates in the workplace. I would get these temporary assignments without much pay; one time, I got one that was about fifteen dollars and He said, "No, I want you to take the one that pays only eight dollars because that is where we are going." Initially, I resented it but when I began to see what the Lord was showing me about the operations of the devil's networks in the workplace, I began to realize that the training that I was getting was worth more than money could ever buy and I began to be excited. I went to several difference companies for the Lord and collected several different anointings and gained understanding about what goes on spiritually in the workplace.

We must not be ignorant of the ways that the devil tries to ensnare us or to get us to agree with him for our own destruction. We have to be discerning and be alert to his wicked devices. As we saw in the case of the pregnant lady above, some of the ways that he tries to ensnare us are with our words, our beliefs, what we see and who we partner or associate with. They can become the legal or technical grounds that the devil uses to contend with us. Let us look at each of these and see how the devil uses them against us.

Our Words:

Our words are powerful and the devil knows this. He is legalistic and always tries to find ways to get to you into a covenant with your words. For example, when we have just finished worshiping God and we are on fire, we are high and soaring like the eagles, he comes through someone or through a phone call to get you to say something that will under mind your positive confessions or get you to speak words that will give him an access to you anytime he wants. If you are not discerning, you can come into agreement with him through a conversation or promise that locks you into a place where God cannot move for you because of the covenant they represent. He knows just who to send that will get you to come into the covenant agreement that he wants. If he is successful, things will start to go contrary to how they were supposed to go or how they started out going and you will pray and get all your friends and everybody you know to pray and nothing moves or changes. Why, because you had ignorantly given the devil a legal ground or a technicality (an ace) to use against you.

In some sports, they have what they call **"TKO"** meaning a **Technical Knock Out**. It is like the ACE in a card game. I like to give the devil a TKO all the time because when he brings something against me, I have learned to run to the Lord and ask, "Lord, what is the Word that destroys this devil's plan?" Once I get the Word and I speak it, I will watch the devil get angry as he gets up to leave. God wants us to be victorious in every circumstance. There are times that I will hear God the Father say to the devil, "Have you considered my servant …?" I will say to Him, "Why Lord, can't you just leave well enough alone?" I will ask Him if the devil is really coming and He will say, "Oh yes, but he better not find anything in you." I will immediately begin to cancel every negative confession that I had made and to repent of anything that I have thought or done that is ungodly.

This is why I use the cleansing prayers in my prayer book to cleanse myself of every word that I have spoken that is contrary to the Word of the Lord. I pluck them up because when the devil is coming, he is frantically looking for what you have said, what have you done and where you have gone that you had no business going that he can use against you. Because we are not careful to watch what we say and what we do, we just arm the devil against us every which way. Since I discovered that this is one of the reasons why God does not allow us to demonstrate His power the way and to the extent that we could, I made up my mind not to make so many ungodly covenants with my words. You will learn that words are very expensive when you see their impact in the realm of the spirit. As a result, I am very, very slow to give a promise. For example, if somebody says to me, "I will see you tomorrow," I may not say a word and you might be wondering what is going on with me because I will look at you but if I am not sure that I will see you tomorrow, I may say, "Maybe." It may seem like a very simple thing but if God has a place for me to be tomorrow and I have already said "yes" to you, the devil can use that verbal commitment (covenant) to sabotage my going to the new place that God has for me. We must learn to say "God willing" to some requests.

You find that although we are born again, we are partaking of Gods divine nature, we are tapping into the realm of the spirit and we are enjoying His divine presence, yet when the devil comes once in a while or most times in a lot of Christians' lives, he is still able to have one up on them. One of the ways the devil does that is through your words. Therefore, if you do not want him to have any "legalities or technicalities" against you, then you need to make sure that your words line up with the Word of the Lord. Make sure that your confessions line up with what God has said about you because if they do not, you just may give the devil a legal ground to set you back.

Some people's tongues and words are their worst enemies. As I said before, Christianity is a confession. You believed in Christ, you spoke your belief and you became a Christian.

"That **if thou shalt confess with thy mouth the Lord Jesus, and shalt believe in thine heart that God hath raised him from the dead, thou shalt be saved**" (Romans 10:9).

What we speak or declare over ourselves determines what we get in life or the outcome of our situations. Our negative or ignorant words give the devil the most effective legal ground against us. We must get the mind of Christ on any issue or subject before we speak. **The most difficult people to help in Christendom are people with a negative tongue.** They will erase your prayers for them with one negative word or confession. Their tongue is nothing but a mulching machine. They will mulch even your words of encouragement to them.

There are people you pray for and at the end of praying for them they say, "Oh yes, I am just hoping that God will do it." They did not have faith and it came out of their mouth and for some other people they are just negative, negative and negative about everything.

A lot of people have died because of their negative confessions with their mouth. During one of my employments in one of the various offices, I worked with a lady whose mother passed away and because of it, she dropped out of church. She was angry with God for taking her mother and she did not want anything to do with the church. One day, the Lord opened the door for me to minister to her and she went on and on about how unfair God had been to her by taking her mother from her because they were best friends. As she spoke, the Lord was so angry and He said, "Ask her what her mother is doing for me in heaven that Jesus cannot do for me?" So I said to her, God said to ask you just what in the world you think He needed your mother so much in heaven to do for Him that Jesus cannot do for Him that He had to pluck your mother from the earth prematurely to go to heaven? He said, ask her what was her mother's confession when she was alive? When I did, her eyes got big and she said, "Oh my God, she always spoke death over herself."

Her mother was like Fred Stanford in the TV program *Stanford and Sons*, always having the "big one" (heart attack). Did he not have the "big one?" He had a heart attack because that was his confession. According to this lady, her mother always told her children that they will drive her to the grave early or that they will give her a heart attack. She saw herself as going to the grave early and she spoke it over herself. True to her words, she went to the grave early. No prayer could have helped her because of the power of her own words. With her words, she gave the devil a legal ground or a technicality that he can use to take her out anytime he wanted and he did. The devil wants to use your own words to knock you out just like a boxer does with a powerful punch when he needs a technical knock out.

When the devil comes to check out a person, he is looking to see what he can use to pull the rug out from under the person. As I said earlier, he is looking for what the person has said or what the person's parents have said over the person or what someone had said that was ungodly that the person came into agreement with. Therefore, when you begin to understand that he is a legalistic entity, you begin to know the value of your words and to understand that your words are very costly. The closer you are to the Lord, the more you will know the power and the cost of your words. You will be slow to speak and quick to hear because when people are trying to bring you into something that is going to be a hindrance to you, you can discern it and withdraw from the people.

Most of the time when people are talking to me, I say "I hear you." I do not say "yes." When I say I hear you, I mean that I understand that is where you are. If I do not have to agree with you, I do not say "yes" because the Bible told us not be a partaker of other people's sins.

> "...**<u>Neither be partaker of other men's sins</u>: keep thyself pure**" (1 Timothy 5:22).

I have paid a lot of price in my life because I was one who was quick to put my two cents in about family problems or family issues. As a result, whenever the Lord revealed a curse that was sent against me or that came down against me, it was usually as a result of something that I said, came into agreement with or where I had put my little two cents in that I had no business.

Now when somebody tells me something in my family or about their family, I just pray. I will pray for them but I am not getting into agreement with them. I will tell them what the Bible said or I will tell them what the Word of the Lord said but they will not get an agreement out of me. A lot of us fight battles that are not even battles that we should be concerning ourselves with but battles that were laid up for us by our parents or their parents with their words.

As I said before, a lot of people confess negatives things over themselves and over their children and by so doing, they make it impossible to help them through prayer. There is a grandmother that I know who always asks for prayer to remove hell, death and destruction from her son and his daughter. The problem is, right after praying for her son and his daughter to remove the hell, death and destruction; she will immediately reinstate the hell, death and destruction over them with the next words out of her mouth. She uses her tongue to totally erase the prayers and their answers by telling you all over again how that her son and his daughter are plagued by hell, death and destruction. You cannot help her son and his daughter until she is willing to change her confession over them but meanwhile her son sits in prison.

Our Beliefs:

Our beliefs also serve as legal and technical grounds for the devil to resist us or steal from us because our beliefs affect our thinking. The Bible says in **Proverbs 23:7** that:

"For as he thinketh in his heart, so is he: Eat and drink, saith he to thee; but his heart is not with thee."

The devil is not after your spirit but after your mind and body. He wants you to learn his negative way of thinking so that he can defeat you. He knows that what you believe controls your actions and that wrong beliefs will produce a wrong course of action in your life.

Your religious beliefs and your general beliefs in life can give the devil a legal ground or a legal case against you and he can always use them to knock you out technically whenever he wants to. Therefore, when you renounce your former wrong religious beliefs, worship or doctrine, you need to pluck up the spirit and cast it out of your life because if not, the devil will try to use them against you. I was shocked that although I am preaching the Gospel and God is using me to deliver people from various forms of afflictions up until two months ago, I was still wrestling with the spirit of Islam!

One day, I entered into my bathroom and the Islamic spirit was quoting the Koran; it was just reciting the Koran as I used to do when I was little and it tried to feed it into my mind forcefully. When I was living with my cousin as a little girl, we had an Islamic instructor that came on Fridays to teach us the Koran. I immediately realized that although I had renounced Islam, there was still an open door into my life to the spirit of the Koran that I had not addressed. Until the day of this event, I had not done anything about the Islamic classes that I had attended and the Koran passages that I had memorized as a child. I had not withdrawn myself from the Islamic school and I had not taken back the permission that I gave to the Islamic instructor to teach me the Koran.

I had to reclaim and dedicate my Fridays to the Lord and I had to declare that Fridays are no longer days for me to learn the Koran. I verbally renounced the Islamic instructor and the Koran passages that I had learned and I came out of the Islamic classroom. I took back the permission that my grandfather, my cousin and I had given to the Islamic instructor to teach me anything and I never heard from that spirit again. When a person's religious beliefs are wrong, the devil will use them to lock up that person and whenever he needs a technical knockout in the person's life, he will use the wrong beliefs to harass, contend or defeat the person. This is why we all have to understand how he uses our wrong beliefs against us.

What We See and Dream:

God shows us visions and dreams in order to get us to agree with His plans and purpose for ourlives. His plans for us are stated in **Jeremiah 29:11**:

> **"For I know the thoughts that I think toward you, saith the LORD, <u>thoughts of peace, and not of evil</u>, <u>to give you an expected end</u>."**

This is the same reason that the devil will show a person a vision or a dream. He too wants us to agree with his evil plans for ourlives. The Lord Jesus told us about the devil's plans for us in **John 10:10**:

> **"<u>The thief cometh not, but for to steal, and to kill, and to destroy</u>: I am come that they might have life, and that they might have it more abundantly."**

As I stated before, the spiritual principle is to get a man or a woman to agree on earth for a spiritual plan to be manifested in earth either by God or by the devil. Therefore our tongues are in high demand because God wants our tongues and the devil wants our tongues but we all get to choose who to give our tongues to.

I teach on visions and dreams and it is amazing how many people the devil can deceive with a false dream or a false vision. They would seem religion or godly but when you analyze them; you will see that they are nothing but a cleverly disguised attempt by the devil to get the people to agree with him for their own destruction. He wants to back you into a little corner and get you into an agreement with him so that everything else that you want the Lord to do for you cannot be accomplished because of the agreement you have with him. This is why you have to make sure that what you are dreaming and what you are seeing (visions) line up with the Word of the Lord before you speak it out.

The Bible tells us that the power to speak life and the power to speak death are in the tongue:

"Death and life are in the power of the tongue: and they that love it shall eat the fruit thereof" (Proverbs 18:21).

Most people immediately share with their friends and relatives the things that they dreamed or saw in a vision. Someone was sharing with me recently about a dream that they had in which they had no face because something had taken away part of their face. You have to be careful how you receive some thing like that because as we saw in the scripture in Jeremiah 29:11 above, God's plans for us are not evil but good; He does not destroy us or give us evil. It is the devil that wants a person to receive the evil plan that he has for the person. Therefore, when a dream does not speak God's plans and purpose for your life, do not claim the dream.

Familiar spirits mimic the people that they are trying to deceive by appearing in the people's dreams. They come around in your dream and they pretend to be "you" doing all the things that they show you in the dream but the next time you see "you" in an evil dream, look at the image very closely because if it is not an image that God has sent to you, there will be something about "the you" in that dream that the familiar spirit cannot effectively mimic.

You might see "yourself" moving in the dream in a way that you do not normally move or acting in a way that you do not normally act and you might be thinking, I do not do that in real life. Why? Because the devil is trying to sell you an image of "you" and that image you saw in the dream was not the real you until you said with your own mouth that it was you!

Once you confess that you are the one you saw in the dream, the devil can bring to pass the condition that he showed you in the dream because you signed for the evil package with your mouth. This is why you never claim to be the person in the dream until you are sure that it is a dream from God.

I told you that the **spiritual law** is that two must agree with heaven or with the devil for something to happen on earth. Therefore, a man or a woman has to come into agreement with what is going on either in God's heaven or with what the devil has laid up in the second heaven in order to see the result. God will give you a dream and He will give you a vision. The devil will also give you a dream or he will give you a vision. Why? Because they both need someone to speak out their plans. One of the things that the Lord showed me is that the devil has no tongue of his own. The reason is because if you read chapter 2 of the book of Job, you will see that he was rude to God so when Jesus defeated him, He pulled out the devil's tongue. This is why he cannot speak directly to you but wars with you in your mind; you will never hear the devil talk to you directly but he can replay in your head the ungodly or wicked things that your parents, your relatives and other people have said to you. Again, this is why you must know who is talking to you in a vision or in a dream (God or the devil) before you come into agreement with it.

God Is the First Source of Your Visions and Dreams:

In my vision and dreams manual titled: ***A Teacher's Manual on Visions and Dreams***, page 53, I outlined how that your visions and dreams can only come from three possible sources. The first source of a dream is God because God gave us this sovereign promise in **Joel 2:28**:

> "And it shall come to pass afterward, that <u>I will pour out my spirit upon all flesh</u>; and <u>your sons and your daughters shall prophesy, your old men shall dream dreams, your young men shall see visions</u>."

It is a sovereign promise to all mankind. Therefore, the criterion for having a dream or a vision is to be a human being. Never presume that unbelievers (none Christians) cannot have a dream or see a vision because they do. The only thing that they lack is an understanding of the dream or vision because it takes the Holy Spirit to reveal or give the understanding. Before we got saved, the Holy Bible was just another book to most of us or worst still it was a book that only fanatics read. Others have probably read the Bible once, twice or sometimes and it really did not mean that much to them but once a person gets born again, the Holy Bible comes alive to the person when he or she reads it because the person's spirit is lighted by the Holy Spirit. From there on, when the person picks up the Holy Bible, it talks back to the person because the Spirit of God will activate the Words in the Bible and He will minister to the person's spirit with the Words.

Many people are too busy during the day for God to talk to because they simply do not have the time to stop and seek Him in order to hear Him. He in turn, tries to speak to people and their busy schedules make them shut Him out. Therefore, He waits until night time to give people night visions or dreams. This is why **Job 33:14-16** says:

> "For <u>God speaketh once, yea twice, yet man perceiveth it not. In a dream, in a vision of the night, when deep sleep falleth</u> upon men, in slumberings upon the bed; <u>Then he openeth the ears of men</u> *(He gives a dream or night vision)*, **and sealeth their instruction."**

A lot of us, especially in western nations are very busy people. Some people only pray in their cars because they will tell you that it is where they can spend their quite time because they are too busy. Because of their busy schedules, they probably do not have time for praise and worship of God nor do they put themselves in a position where they can get a vision; so God waits until they go to sleep so that He can give them instructions, warnings, or what He has for them.

This is why **Job 33:17-18** says:

"That he may withdraw man from his purpose, and hide pride from man. He keepeth back his soul from the pit, and his life from perishing by the sword *(warning)."*

If you look in the book of Genesis, you will see how God used series of dreams to tell Joseph about his future and eventually when it was time for Joseph to be promoted, God gave the most powerful king on earth in those days (Pharaoh) a dream that only Joseph could interpret. God used the gift of understanding visions and dreams to open the door for Joseph and He did the same thing for the Prophet Daniel in Babylon. You can read about Joseph and Daniel in Genesis Chapters 37- 41 and Daniel Chapter 2.

Visions and dreams are tools that God uses today to speak with people. They are tangible ways of communication by God and the devil. God can have someone prophesy over you, give you a rhema word (the Word of God for you now) while you are reading the Bible and He can talk to you in a dream or a vision. You cannot discount any of them or think that they are just figments of your imagination (unless it is one of those pizza dreams) but what you do is learn how to interpret your visions and dreams correctly. If you do not, you can give the devil a legal or technical ground to sabotage you or stop what you have started to build; especially if you have been confessing the false dreams the devil has been giving to you. The Bible says in **Matthew 18:16** that out of the mouth of two or three witnesses every word is established:

> **"...In the mouth of two or three witnesses every word may be established."**

The minute you call your friend and you share with him or her the false dream from the devil and the two of you agree that you were the person in the dream, then, the two of you have just established the dream with your words. This is dangerous when it comes to speaking dreams or visions that are not from God. Therefore, make sure that your visions and dreams are from God before you share them with anyone.

The Devil Is the Second Source of Your Visions and Dreams:

As you can already guess, the second source of your visions or dreams is the devil himself. He will give them to you for the purposes that I just told you above. He does not want you to succeed, he wants you to fail, he wants you sick and he wants you dead. When you see yourself going from a car to a bicycle in a dream, do not call your best friend and say, "I had this strange dream; I had this Cadillac and next thing I know, I was on this bike and I went from a paved road to a gravel road. The scene changed and I did not know where I was and I woke up. I do not remember the rest of the dream." This is a classic dream of the devil's attempt to get you to agree for demotion.

Therefore, when you wake up, an holy indignation should rise up in you and you should tell the devil that you are not of those that go backwards. Tell him that you do not agree with him to demote you and begin to claim God's promotion in every area of your life.

The Bible says in **Proverbs 4:18** that the path of the righteous is like a shinning light and it shines more and more unto the perfect day. Therefore, do not let the devil deceive you to receive his demotion and backward plans.

> **"But the path of the just is as the shining light, that shineth more and more unto the perfect day."**

If you own a beautiful home and the devil takes you to your grandmother's house that is falling down or takes you to a place that represents your past with its ungodliness, do not wake up in the morning and call your best friend and say, "I just dreamed today that I was back at my grandmother's house and me and my cousins were having all these arguments and…" Instead, you should tell the devil that you have been redeemed and you do not go backward. That is why the Bible said let the redeemed of the Lord say so. Let him know that you have been redeemed.

> **"Let the redeemed of the LORD say so, whom he hath redeemed from the hand of the enemy…"** (Psalm 107:2).

You Are the Third Source of Your Visions and Dreams:

The third source of your visions and dreams is yourself. The reason "yourself" will give you a dream or a vision is because your subconscious self loves you. You are your own "one man umpire" and if everybody else is against you, your subconscious self loves you. Therefore, when you like or desire something intensely, your subconscious self wants to satisfy your desire so when you go to sleep, it will create scenarios in which your heart's desire is being satisfied. It wants to make you feel better. For instance, if it is a particular lady that you love and desire, your subconscious self will create a dream in which you see you and the lady carrying on in a loving way but you have to be careful that you do not wake up in the morning and go, "God has shown me that the lady is my wife" because it was nothing but a self dream! God is not obligated to bring a dream that is the result of your heart deceiving you to pass. Self dreams never manifest.

God wants us to have His wisdom so that we can determine when God is the one talking to us in a dream, when the devil is the one talking or if it is "self" trying to help us get what we desire. This is why you need to know the sources of your visions and dreams and learn how to tell who is speaking to you with them. It is not enough for a spirit to speak to you but what the spirit says to you must line up with the Word of God because you want to embrace God's plans and purposes for you but you also want to avoid the devil's legalities and technicalities against you.

For more information on how to understand and interpret your visions and dreams, see my manual and textbook titled: ***A Teacher's Manual on Visions and Dreams***, and ***Keys to Understanding Your Visions and Dreams.*** The manual contains actual lessons for teaching the visions and dreams class and the textbook will give you all the detailed teachings on them. These are very valuable materials for anyone desiring to better understand their visions and dreams.

Partnership or Association:

It matters who you go into partnership with or who you associate with in your personal or business relationships because a partner/associate can either bring you a blessing or cause you to suffer loss. The following are examples of partnerships or associates in the Bible that either were a hindrance or a blessing.

1. **Abraham and Lot:** If you remember, Abraham was called of the Lord to leave his people. One of the things that he did was add a little bit to the Lord's instruction of "leave your people." He took Lot along with him and Lot caused him some hardship along the way. Lot got into trouble and Abraham had to go to war to rescue him and Lot's employees quarreled so much with Abraham's employees to the point that Abraham finally decided to let Lot go away from him. Lot chose the seemingly best part of the land but what happened all the while Lot was with Abraham was that Abraham did not get God's specific instruction concerning his future until Lot separated from him! God waited until Abraham was willing to let Lot go and as soon as Lot left, God spoke to Abraham. We see this in **Genesis 13:14**:

> "**And the LORD said unto Abram, after that Lot was separated from him**, Lift up now thine eyes, and look from the place where thou art northward, and southward, and eastward, and westward."

I was amazed that the scripture said **that the Lord spoke to Abram after Lot was separated from him.** Do you know how many people have hindered their blessings by having people in their lives that God has not approved? God waited to remind Abraham about His plan for him until Lot was gone away from him. As soon as Lot was gone, He tells Abraham, look to the north, to the south, to the east and to the west for as far as you can see; that have I given unto you. There are some things that God will wait for you to do before He can manifest His promises in your life. Primary among them is who you partner or associate with. He told me some years ago that He did not send me to win a popularity contest and that I needed to separate from the people that were my so called "friends" then. To illustrate His point, He told me to look in **Isaiah 51:2.** It says:

> "**Look unto Abraham your father, and unto Sarah that bare you: for I called him alone, and blessed him, and increased him.**"

God called Abraham alone and not Abraham and Lot but Abraham was not aware of this specific call and so he spent many years in hardship because he had Lot with him. Do you know how many people have a "Lot" in their lives contrary to God's will? They are only delaying the manifestation of their blessings because as you can see in the case of Abraham, as long as he had Lot with him, he had trouble and delayed blessings.

2. **The Lord and Judas:** Another example of the effect of a partner or an associate in scripture is the case of the Lord Jesus and Judas Iscariot in **Matthew 26:14-16**:

> "**Then one of the twelve, called Judas Iscariot, went unto the chief priests, *15* And said unto them,**

What will ye give me, and I will deliver him unto you? And they covenanted with him for thirty pieces of silver. *16* **And from that time he sought opportunity to betray him."**

When you look at the Lord Jesus, you will notice that whenever the Pharisees, the Scribes and the Sadducees sought to trap, stone or kill Him, scripture says, "He passing through the midst of them went His way." The Lord showed me that He did not have any open doors in His life for the devil to bring death or destruction against Him so they could not touch Him. He would just walk away safely:

"And all they in the synagogue, when they heard these things, were filled with wrath, *29* **And rose up, and thrust him out of the city, and led him unto the brow of the hill whereon their city was built, that they might cast him down headlong.** *30* ***But he passing through the midst of them went his way***" (Luke 4:28-30).

The Sanhedrin could not get to the Lord to harm Him but the day the Lord made a covenant with Judas Iscariot, there was an open door to Him and the devil knew it. He immediately used Judas to betray Him. The Lord was well aware of what the covenant with Judas meant for Him hence He said during His last dinner with the disciples, "One of you (my covenant brethren) is going to betray Me." He knew that He had become vulnerable because of the covenant of brotherhood (partnership) with them and that the devil was going to use Judas to get to Him. It was already foretold in scripture that it was the way it would happen.

From this you can see how your associate or partner, in this case a covenant brother can make you vulnerable to the devil. For a mere thirty pieces of silver, Judas sold out Jesus. Today, we all benefit from the blessing of being in a covenant (partnership) with the Lord. As a result, of the partnership that we have with the Lord, we can enjoy the Abrahamic covenant blessings.

3. **David and Jonathan:** If you look at David and Jonathan, you will again see the importance of association and partnership. David was anointed king but Saul was the reigning king and it took the words from Jonathan's mouth to deliver the kingdom to David. If you look at **1 Samuel 18:3-4,** you will see the transaction between David and Jonathan:

> **"Then Jonathan and David made a covenant, because he loved him as his own soul. *4* And Jonathan stripped himself of the robe that was upon him, and gave it to David, and his garments, even to his sword, and to his bow, and to his girdle."**

Remember how Esau gave his birthright to Jacob? Esau willingly relinquished it to Jacob. Jonathan stripped himself of his royalty and he placed them on David. Talk about prophetic demonstration; if you listen to him, you will notice that at the end he said to David, "I know that you are going to be king." See how our words matter? He also said, my father also knows that you are going to be king and I will stand next to you. In other words, he willingly removed himself physically from the royal lineage and from the birthright of kingship.

In **1 Samuel 23:17,** Jonathan single handedly delivered the kingdom to David:

> **"And he** (Jonathan) **said unto him** (David)**, Fear not: for the hand of Saul my father shall not find thee; <u>and thou shalt be king over Israel, and I shall be next unto thee; and that also Saul my father knoweth</u>."**

God would have waited for Saul to live, reign and die and somehow worked it out so that David can become king but Jonathan delivered it up. Jonathan died because although he relinquished the throne unto David, he did not keep his promise to stand by David. Instead, he went back to stand with his father, King Saul and died with him on the battle field. He would have lived had he stayed with David as he promised. It matters what we say because the Word of the Lord would have come to pass in David's life but Jonathan hasted the fulfillment of the prophecy by what he said and what he did.

Although like all the other children of Israel, David was a descendant of Abraham, he was not from any kingship lineage and there was no royal blood in him but it took Jonathan to bestow the honor and dignity of royalty upon him so that God's Word over David could come to pass. You can see the importance of the words and the actions of Jonathan and their effects in David's life. It worked out good for David because it was the Lord's will for him to be the next king. We all have to be careful about who we partnership with and what we say because we can use them to arm or give the devil legal grounds and technicalities against us.

4. <u>**Paul and Silas:**</u> in **Acts 16:25-26:**
   Also, we can see how the partnership of the Apostle Paul and Silas had a profound effect in their lives and in the lives of their fellow prisoners. They could have come together to murmur and complain but instead, they both decided to pray, praise and worship God. As a result, God responded by opening the prison doors and setting them and all the other prisoners free!

   "And at midnight Paul and Silas prayed, and sang praises unto God: and the prisoners heard them. *26* <u>And suddenly there was a great earthquake, so that the foundations of the prison were shaken: and immediately all the doors were opened, and every one's bands were loosed</u>."

Yes, a partner can influence your course of action for good or bad. Therefore, choose godly partners.

Vision Killers:

There are some people that I call visions killers and you need to be able to recognize the vision killers in your life. They are those who engage in envy, jealousy, rivalries and competition with you. Vision killers are people that come around you as your friends, business affiliates, associates, partners and social buddies. They can be your spiritual associates also. They will kill your vision if you do not get divine wisdom concerning them or disengage yourself from association with them. We are told in the **Song of Solomon 8:6** that jealousy is cruel:

> **"Set me as a seal upon thine heart, as a seal upon thine arm: for love is strong as death; <u>jealousy is cruel as the grave</u>: <u>the coals thereof are coals of fire, which hath a most vehement flame.</u>"**

Jealousy is the number one vision killer among "friends." Therefore we must be careful of those who walk in jealousy towards us and also we must avoid walking in jealousy towards others. The devil will use such people to kill your God-given vision if you continue to allow them access into your life. Their jealousy will become a tool in the hand of the devil against you.

In one of my books titled, *Effective Prayers for Various Situations, Volume I,* I included a *"Prayer to Remove Unfriendly Friends"* and a *"Prayer to Remove the Spirit of Jealousy"* from your life. We all need to know who we are in relationship with and who we allow to have a relationship with us. On the surface, they may seem to be your friends but inwardly, they do not have your best interest and they will secretly rejoice when bad things happen to you. As the saying goes, "With such friends, who needs enemies?" Therefore, do not let people that have jealousy, rivalry, competition and envy in their hearts come around you. They will kill your vision if you do not extricate yourself from them. You can easily identify such among your "friends" because whatever you own is the next thing that they want to own and if you put on something, that is the next thing that they also want to put on. If you share your vision with them or tell them what you want to do next, some of them will just outright resent you. The devil will ride on the jealousy in their hearts against you and use it to attack and destroy whatever you share with them.

I own a publishing company called, **To His Glory Publishing Company, Inc.**, and we publish books for people and place them on Amazon.com, Barnesandnoble.com and other online bookstores. One of the things that I say to my new authors when they publish their first book is not to be surprised if some of the people that they think are going to be happy for them are not. I usually tell them that some people will resent them or actually stop talking to them the minute they start stepping out as a published authors. I experienced it when I published my first book and many of my authors have also experienced it with their relatives, friends and colleagues. Some people just do not know how to be happy for another person when something good happens to the person.

An Experience with a Jealous "Friend":

I remember some years ago, I had gone through my "major wilderness experience" and I believed I was coming out of my wilderness and I had three hundred and fifty dollars in my bank account. This was a very good thing for me because I had not been able to save for about three years before this time. It was a breakthrough experience for me to have the savings and there was a lady I knew who was also going through a rough financial time in her life. I had tried to help her but I finally had to remove myself from her because I discerned that it was not spiritually healthy for me to have her in my life. The following is an account of my last dealings with her.

> *One day, I went walking in the evening and I noticed that her car had not moved; you know how you go by a car and you see a piece of leaf or stick by one of the tires. As I went by the next day, I again noticed that the leaf or stick was still by the tire which*

is an indication that the car had not been moved. This went on for days and my first thought was that she was out of town but I noticed that her lights were on at night so I just wondered what was up with her. About five days later, she came knocking on my door and she informed me that she had shut herself in with the Lord for days to seek the Lord concerning her rent. She then informed me that the Lord told her to come to me and I asked her how much she needed to complete her rent and she said $300.

I was angry at the Lord because He alone knew that I had finally managed to save up $350 and now He wants me to give $300 of it to this lady. I actually went as far as asking the Lord if He thought that I was allergic to having money in my bank account. I was much displeased with Him but I knew that I had to obey the Lord because I had a witness in my spirit that I was supposed to give her the money. She told me she would pay me back in about three weeks. I told her to come with me to the bank and I withdrew the money and I gave it to her. This happened on a weekday. The next Sunday, I was in church and during praise and worship, the Lord told me not to ask the lady to pay me back the $300 dollars! Needless to say that I was not very happy with the Lord about it. I wanted to know what I had done wrong that made Him give away the little that I have and I am not to ask for it back.

I went to her and told her that the Lord said that she is not to pay me back. I watched as she danced about praising God for His faithfulness to her and meanwhile, I felt that I was on the losing end of the deal with God. I was not a happy camper about what the Lord had done to me but He and I had come a long way so I had to cheer up and trust Him. Could you believe that when I went to bed that night, *the Lord gave me a vision of this same lady declaring war against me and acting very angry towards me? She was throwing me boxing punches and I was shocked that she was acting that way towards me after I had helped her.*

I cried out to the Lord to reveal to me why she was so hostile towards me after I had helped her. The Lord said it was because as long as she thought that the two of us were struggling financially, she was fine but since I was able to give her $300 without asking for it back, she thinks that things are now very good for me and jealousy has risen up in her against me. This was why I was seeing her trying to kick and box me in the realm of the spirit. I thought it was sad that she reacted the way she did because little did she know that she left me with only fifty dollars in my bank account after I gave her the $300.

God told me that when He shows me that a person is walking in jealousy towards me, I am to cut the person loose from my life because the person is a vision killer. Therefore, I say to you that when you discern that someone is walking in jealousy, in rivalry and in competition with you, you need to cut the person loose. You do not want the person to become an avenue for the devil to come against you and destroy what you are trying to build.

Because we are talking about the devil's legalities and technicalities against us, I say again, that it is critical that we know how the enemy operates, how God operates and how we are supposed to operate in order to avoid giving the devil legal grounds against us. It will also help us to walk in prosperity and in the covenant blessings that Christ purchased for us. After reading this book, you should apply what you have learned in your life so that you can change your circumstances and begin to walk in victory.

We can have many church services, conferences and seminars and they are all good but we also need life changing principles and a good understanding of how to apply God's spiritual principles so that we can walk victoriously in life. It is the reason why I wrote this book on how to understand the power of covenant and how to use covenants in our lives. You can actually look at your life and personally identify where your weak points are, identify what the devil has been using against you and your family so that you can repent and renounce the covenant as well as purpose to do things differently from now on. Some people have a gift of compassion and when they use this gift based solely on their emotions, the devil can come in and pervert it. Because they do not know how to be led by the Holy Spirit, they can begin to feel that it is their calling to go out there and be everything to everybody. The devil will begin to harass them with condemnation if they do not continue to over burden themselves with their self-appointed and good intentions type works.

Therefore, do not let the devil pervert your gift of compassion or mercy by allowing him to condemn you when you do not do certain things. What God wants from us is to be a people that have His wisdom, know His Word and correctly apply it in our lives. To me, if all that you get from reading this book is how to correctly apply God's covenant in your life, I would have done my job and I thank the Lord because it will go along way to help you pray and petition God correctly as well as keep you safe from the devil's legalities and technicalities.

Example of How the Devil Hinders with a Covenant:

This section of the book shows examples of how the devil can use covenants to hinder people. You can image someone who is born again, Spirit-filled and on fire for the Lord. This person is in church every time the door opens and he or she is really trying to live life according to the Word of God but he or she cannot seem to shake off the negative things that seem to plague him or her. This person may not be aware that his or her great grandfather was a psychic or a Freemason and had made an evil covenant with the devil on his or her behalf. As a result of this outstanding evil covenant, this person can be right on in giving the Word of the Lord or prophesying, he or she can quote the Bible and pray but when you look at his or her life, there are the spirits of lack, mental affliction or harassment, health problems in areas of breathing and a general state of destitution.

It is as though money, favor, good health, etc., seems to run away from him or her. This person is always struggling with one thing or another and people constantly have to help him or her out but when you take a good look at this person, you are baffled because he or she seems to be a very committed Christian but when it comes to prosperity, this person is living way below what God has for him or her. One of the major reasons for this is because there is an active covenant through past Freemason involvement or through psychic activities in the family that gives the devil access to contend with this person in the area of prosperity.

A Vision of the Spirits of Hindrances:

The Lord showed me a night vision in which there was a warehouse and in this warehouse was everything that people had prayed for. The provisions were delivered to this warehouse for everyone who had asked and everyone was supposed to go into this warehouse and pick up their package because the packages have the owner's name on them. What each person was supposed to do was just walk in and pick up the package that belongs to him or her. The Lord took me to the scene and I was surprised to see that nobody was going into the warehouse or coming out with anything even though the warehouse was full of things for the people. Therefore, I went closer and I saw that there was a table set up in front of the warehouse and there were about four guys sitting on this table and they had these large, green computer-print-out sheets that seem to scroll forever. I noticed that what they were doing was screening anyone who wanted to go into the warehouse and if they find your name on their computer list, you cannot go in.

As a result, there was a very long line because just about everyone had their name on the list. These guys were very strict not to let anyone whose name was on their list into the warehouse. I came to the table in this vision and I began to yell to everyone on the line that they do not have to go through the checkpoint at the table because it was an illegal checkpoint. I told them that God did not set up the checkpoint but the devil. I began to tell everyone to go in and pick up their package without stopping at the checkpoint.

I got up from this night vision and I wanted to have an understanding of it from the Lord. The Lord then began to show me that it is the devil that wants to make sure that people's names are on his list so that he can enforce his legal grounds to prevent them from going into the warehouse. This is what the devil does; he looks to see what area you have a covenant with him so that he can hinder you in those areas. When you pray and things are released to you, he comes in and begins to contend with you in areas that you or the generations before you made a covenant with him. His goal is to stop you from receiving your blessings.

Remember how Daniel prayed in **Daniel 10:12-13** and God sent the Angel Gabriel to bring Daniel the answer to his prayers but the Prince of Persia withstood the Angel Gabriel for twenty one days? The Archangel Michael had to come to the Angel Gabriel's aid in order for him to overcome the Prince of Persia and get the answers to the Prophet Daniel.

"Then said he unto me, Fear not, Daniel: for from the first day that thou didst set thine heart to understand, and to chasten thyself before thy God, thy words were heard, and I am come for

> thy words. *13* **But the prince of the kingdom of Persia withstood me one and twenty days: but, lo, Michael, one of the chief princes, came to help me;** and I remained there with the kings of Persia."

Do not be so naive as to believe that the devil will not try to hinder the answers to your prayers. As you can see from the above scripture, the Angel Gabriel was bringing the answers to Daniel's prayers and he was hindered for twenty one days. Can you then imagine what the devil will try to do in the case of someone whose grandparents were steeped into idolatry or who has an active covenant with the devil through their parents or their grandparents? You cannot just walk away or ignore your spiritual roots that are ungodly. You need to pluck them up, you need to root them up, you need to destroy them and you need to begin to build and to plant righteousness and peace in those areas.

One of the things the Lord told me was to "never sow among thorns" because thorns will choke the seed you sowed if you do not root them out first.

> **"For thus saith the LORD to the men of Judah and Jerusalem, Break up your fallow ground, and sow not among thorns"** (Jeremiah 4:3).

A good farmer always goes into a farm and ploughs the ground before he sows anything in the ground. As a result, we are to plow our grounds and we are to prepare it to make sure that that it is good for us to sow into. This is one of the reason that when you read my books, ***Effective Prayers for Various Situations, Volumes I and II***, you will see that I included *prayers to cleanse your life, prayers to cleanse the foundation of your marriage, prayers to reclaims the grounds that were given to the devil by the generations before you and even prayers to cleanse your children that were conceived outside of the marriage covenant.* The reason I did this is because the Lord has taught me that we should not ignore the outstanding evil covenants that are producing negative effects in our lives. For example, a child that was conceived through fornication is already predisposed to have a promiscuous adolescent life. The spirit of fornication and sexual promiscuity were part of the foundation of the conception of the child. If the child wants a victorious and holy living as an adult in this area, he or she will have to pray to cleanse the foundation of his or her conception. If not, the devil will always come in to lord it over his or her life in this area. You can continue to pray for such a person and watch him or her fall into the ungodly lifestyle over and over again. This will change when the covenant made at his or her conception with the spirit of fornication or promiscuity is renounced.

When we look at our families or when we look at our lives, we see tell tales of evil covenants that seek to make our lives difficult or miserable. For example, there are those who cannot receive a dream or who have a dream and cannot remember it. It may not occur to them that the Word of God is right that God is not the author of confusion. Why will God give you a dream and then not give you the ability to remember the dream? It may never occur to them that one major reason that most people cannot remember their dreams is because there is a force that has a primary claim over their spiritual eyes! For instance, a Freemason covenant or a psychic covenant or a witchcraft covenant in your family can block your spiritual eyes from seeing what God has given you because the spiritual eyes in your family have been given over to the devil through the Freemason, psychic or witchcraft covenant.

If you look at the US dollar bill, you will notice that it has an Egyptian Pyramid eye (evil eye) on it and this is a Freemason covenant that blocks the godly eye and only allows the "evil eye" to operate in its victims' lives. It will impair all your spiritual abilities to see into the realm of the spirit if you have been sanctified through your grandparents or your parents to it through the covenant of Freemasonry. It will not allow you to see or remember any good dream. Many people who have an outstanding evil eye covenant with devil often wonder why they cannot see spiritually even though they are born again. Your eyes cannot see spiritually because the devil has primary claim to them and he may be going, "This person's eyes are mine; I alone can show him/her things according to my covenant with them, their father or their grandfather. I was here before they got saved; they invited me into the family and they have not asked me to leave."

As a result, you will be surprised at the ungodly covenants that are in place in the life of one believer. You have the ungodly covenants that you made and the ones from your parents, their parents and their parent's parents. You are dealing with these covenants from both your father and your mother's sides of the family. Worst still, if you are someone whose background is like mine was; from Africa where all we ever knew was idolatry, it is like all hell broke loose against you when you decided to become a born again. Here you are; a new Christian trying to move forward and the devil says, "I know that blood line very well, they are idolaters and I have many doors through which I can go into their lives to hinder them. It is true that he is born again and he can praise God all he wants, but when it comes to finances, prosperity, respect, etc., he will have to contend with me."

Have you ever been in line in a supermarket and everyone was being served and the line seemed to be moving on well until it got to your turn and all of a sudden a cashier or clerk abruptly walked off saying I am closed or became abrasive with you? When such things happen more than twice in a short time period, you need to see a pattern and ask the Lord, "What am I dealing with here? Is there a covenant of disrespect that is making them to cut me off when it is my turn?" Do not ignore the devil's attempts to cut you off or prevent something good from happening to you when it is your turn. Always remember that the people are not your enemies but the spirits that stir them up to act ugly towards you. In response, try peacefully to find someone in management who can correct the wrong but make sure that you address the situation with the Lord so that He can show you how to rebuke the spirit.

As I stated earlier on, when you look at some families, you will see tell tales of evil covenants that are in place in the family. Tell tales such as, unmarriedness; mother never got married and daughter never got married. Mother got pregnant as a teenager and daughter did the same. Little teenage granddaughter is already pregnant and there are other tell tales such as unemployment, imprisonment, poverty, incest, murder, etc., in each generation of the family.

The following story will help you to see how the devil can assign an evil spirit and how we can make a covenant with the evil spirit with our words. I hope that this story will open your eyes and help you to be sympathetic when evil things happen to other people.

Story A:

There was a lady that came to me some time age and she was going through a crisis with her brother, Amos. She told me that her brother was too ashamed to talk to anyone about his crisis and he would not even tell his wife about what happened to him. I asked what happened and she said that her brother, Amos, who is forty five years old, got raped by another man. According to her, he is born again and loves the Lord. He is active in his church and he is against the homosexual life style. One day, he went out to run an errand and he stopped in a local bar for a beer. While he was drinking his beer, the subject of homosexuality came up and he promptly informed the two men at the bar that homosexuality was a sin according to the Word of God. When he stepped away from the bar, one of the men slipped a hallucinogenic pill into his beer and he was not aware of it. Shortly after he finished his beer, he began to get dizzy so he went into the men's room to splash some water on his face. While he was at the sink, the man who put the pill in his beer came in and slammed him to the ground and he was too hallucinated and weak to fight back and the man raped him.

As this lady was telling me about what happened to her brother Amos, I asked her who else in her family had been raped before. From my experience in the deliverance ministry, these things do not just happen. There has to be an open door for the devil to come in and you will also discover as you begin to understand how things happen in the realm of the spirit that such things do not just happen. This is why I wanted to know who else had been raped before him and she said that she was raped many years before. I then asked her what Amos said to her when he heard that she had been raped. I wanted to know the first thing that came out of his mouth when he heard what happened to her. Did he judge you? Did he condemn you for the way you dressed or did he show you sympathy? I wanted to know these things because the Bible says in **Luke 6:38**, ***"Give and it shall be given unto you...For with the same measure that ye mete withal it shall be measured to you again."*** *Her eyes got bigger as she spoke and I began to discern that I was listening to an incident that was brought on because of words of judgment so I said it sounds to me like he brought judgment on himself. She said, "Oh, he said....*

I told her to tell him that he needs to ask her for forgiveness because he did not show her mercy and sympathy when the evil (rape) happened to her. He needs his sister to forgive him for the first words of condemnation and judgment that came out of him against her when she was raped. ***By the same words, he made a covenant with the spirit of rape and then he set himself up to be the victim of the spirit according to Luke 6:38.*** *Since he spoke those words, the spirit has been looming around him waiting for the right opportunity to strike and when the conditions were right at that bar, it did. So, you see that covenants can be made with our words and judgments.*

Story B:

Also, another woman came to one of my classes a few months ago and she said that her thirty year old son tried to rape her sister, his aunt. According to her, she was visiting her mother with her sister and her son also happened to be there in the house. When she and her mother were not home and the sister was home alone with her son, he tried to rape her. I also asked her who was raped before in her family. She told me that she had been raped when she was a young girl. I asked her if she had ever had someone to pray and drive away the spirit of rape from her and she said no. I then informed her about how she had innocently passed the spirit onto her son because the spirit was still in her when she conceived and gave birth to him.

When she got raped as a girl, she got healed physically and emotionally but the spirit of rape that was deposited in her was not driven away from her. As a result, when she got pregnant, she was already a carrier of the spirit of rape and the son picked it up from the womb and when the conditions were right, the spirit surfaced in his life. I told her that she needs to have the spirit first removed from her and then from her son so that they do not establish a lineage of rapist or a lineage in which someone always rapes another in the family.

The devil only operates where people give him opportunity to operate and it is usually through a covenant. You need to look into your lineage and find out what covenants you are dealing with, what covenants are in place in your family and what it is that was done contrary to the Word of God that is now affecting your life negatively. When you begin to recognize the ungodly covenant patterns and you begin to address them, you will start to enjoy tremendous blessings in the areas of your life that were virtually impossible for good things to happen to you before. We all need to really come to that place where we recognize that covenants are very critical to our success and prosperity in life.

Chapter 4

Walking in the Path of Safety

This chapter deals with how to walk in safety with the Lord to avoid the devil's fiery darts and evil plans but I will like to issue a disclaimer right here by stating that the revelations that I share in this book and in all of my books are not the result of being better than anyone else or because I know more than anyone else. It is just because I was more stupid (I think) than most people and I operated in "zeal without knowledge" several times that I got myself into a lot of spiritual trouble and God had to deliver me and give me some spiritual common sense. I needed to know why I was getting into trouble with the Lord, with the devil and with people who were not ready for what I had to share with them. As a result of the Lord's mercy and grace, it looks as thought I have seen so much, been through so much or know so much but it is only because He chose to rescue one that was just too prone to take off and do things without knowledge. I survived by His grace and if I can help others avoid the mistakes that I made, then what I went through was not in vain.

Also, I believe that some of the spiritual common sense that I learned may help others to find God's path of safety sooner than latter in life. There came a day in which God gave David rest from all his enemies round about him and he became free of the stress of having enemies round about him. I believe that God wants this for all of us. David was a warrior and fought battles for many years but one day he came to a place of rest whereby he no longer had to go to war because he entered into God's rest just like the Bible said that he that has entered into God's rest seizes from his own works.

Do Not Go Around the Mountain Again:

Jesus said in **Luke 22:37** that the things that concerns Him had an ending which means both His suffering and every experience that He went through on earth. There is a day that the Lord's sufferings, trials, persecutions, agony etc., came to an end. The end for us does not have to be death because the Lord already paid that price for us.

> **"For I say unto you, that this that is written must yet be accomplished in me, And he was reckoned among the transgressors: <u>for the things concerning me have an end</u>."**

Therefore, there should come a time in a believer's life in which his or her particular trial or trouble should come to an end and we call it breakthrough or getting to the other side. We are not destined to continually go through the same cycle or mountain over and over again without an end in sight. Just like Jesus, the things that concern us must have an end because we are in Him and we are bone of his bones and one Spirit with Him. We are not apart from Him:

> **"For we are <u>members of his body, of his flesh</u>, and <u>of his bones</u>"** (Ephesians 5:30).

> **"But <u>he that is joined unto the Lord is one spirit</u>"** (I Corinthians 6:17).

The Holy Spirit unites us with the Lord so that we are now one with Him. **He paid for us to enjoy the victory that He won for us on the Cross**. He is interested in us walking safely and victoriously. **As a result, I am now going to talk about how to walk safely in the Lord and I call it walking in the path of safety**. By this, I mean how we all can walk with the Lord and not take a hit from the devil. Even when you take a hit, you should not get knocked off and loose your ground, loose your harvest, loose your prosperity or whatever was coming your way.

There is a path and there is a place in God where you can walk safely so that when the devil is coming against you, you have an advantage over him to defeat him. The question is how do you walk with the Lord in the path of safety? You do not have to let the devil knocked you off and make you to start all over again. I want to help you understand how God first deals with us before setting us on this path of safety. He has a process for us all.

God's Wrestling with New Believers:

Most of us come to the Lord having a background of false religions, ungodly ways, ungodly behaviors and a very strong self-will of how we want things done. We have basically been in control of our lives for as far as we can remember but the Lord Jesus wants us to be led by the Holy Spirit and not our flesh. The Lord then proceeds to lay His foundation in our lives so that we can withstand what He is trying to build in our lives in order for us to fulfill our God-given destinies. Because people do not take the time to lay a proper foundation before they go into life changing agreements such as marriage, business partners, legal agreements, etc., they leave room for the devil to come and under mind what they are trying to build.

This is one of the major reasons why you see marriages breakup easily because the foundation was not right. A lot of people get married because they see their potential spouse as the person who will fulfill a need in their lives and when the spouse looses the ability to fulfill that need, the spouse becomes expendable. They convince themselves that the spouse no longer loves them and they move on to another person. Their definition of love is based on material provision and they are not willing to be inconvenienced by any required life changes that might make the marriage work. But God is not like man, He sees all the junk in us when we come to Him and because He loves us, He is willing to invest time in cleaning us up for His glory but He has a process that we must all pass through. Many call it God's crucible or cleansing fire.

In other words, He brings us to a place where He can begin to wrestle with us in order to deliver us from the ungodly things that we had learned and from our very strong self-will. Many of us are very strong in our natural abilities, natural talents and our very own sense of what is right and what is wrong. We also know exactly what we want to do, how we want to do it and when we want it done but God in a firm but loving way wrestles us to the ground to strip us of our self reliance so that we can learn to depend on Him. He wants us to walk by placing our faith in Him and not in ourselves or other people.

God knows that if left alone, we are going to make a havoc of everything that He releases us to do. Therefore, He intentionally takes us into this path that is difficult and hard where He can crucify our flesh and teach us to listen to His instructions. His main goal is to teach us to trust His love and depend on Him for all our needs.

Why the Wilderness?:

We see this in His dealings with the children of Israel. He intentionally led the children of Israel through the wilderness in order to accomplish some things in them. It is outlined in **Deuteronomy 8:2-3 and Deuteronomy 8:15-16** where Moses is talking to the children of Israel about the Lord:

> "<u>Who led thee through that great and terrible wilderness</u>, <u>wherein were fiery serpents</u>, and <u>scorpions</u>, and <u>drought</u>, where there was <u>no water</u>; who brought thee forth water out of the rock of flint; *16* Who fed thee in the wilderness with manna, which thy fathers knew not, <u>that he might humble thee</u>, and <u>that he might prove thee, to do thee good at thy latter end</u>."

The Lord knew it was a great and terrible wilderness and He hand picked it for the children of Israel. There was an easier way to get from Egypt into Judea but He looked for this "great and terrible wilderness" that had fiery serpents, scorpions and drought as the right place where He could accomplish His plans and purposes in the children of Israel. Why did He take them through the terrible wilderness? He had to teach them to depend on Him and His Word for their lives. They must have faith and trust in His love. This is truly a humbling experience.

> "**And thou shalt remember all the way which the LORD thy God led thee these forty years in the wilderness, to humble thee,** and **to prove thee, to know what was in thine heart, whether thou wouldest keep his commandments, or no**. *3* **And he humbled thee, and suffered thee to hunger,** and fed thee with manna, which thou knewest not, neither did thy fathers know; **that he might make thee know that man doth not live by bread only, but by every word that proceedeth out of the mouth of the LORD doth man live**."

Everyone that comes to God must learn to live by the Word of God and lean to put his or her trust in Him. **We are to know Him and His ways but many of us do not know Him or His ways until we are born again and He then begins the process of teaching us about Himself, His Word and His ways. This is very difficult for us because His ways are so different from our ways and His Word goes against our self-will.** One of the things that the scripture tells us in **Psalm 103:7** is that Moses knew the ways of the Lord but the children of Israel only knew His acts:

> "**He made known his ways unto Moses**, his acts unto the children of Israel."

If you are a person that does not know the ways of the Lord and all you know is His acts, you are in for a shock because His ways do not appeal to our senses or make sense to us most times. Instead, they sometimes seem rather cruel and we feel abandoned by Him at this state because we are going through so many difficult things and He seems very slow in responding. Some might wonder if He will ever respond at all. He will allow you to go through so much that you will actually begin to wonder if He really loves you the way the Bible says. You begin to say to yourself; if He is love, why is He letting me go through all of this stuff? He leads us by His Spirit but I do not believe that God actually brings anything against us as He leads us, but He will allow certain things to happen to us. I believe that all He does is take His hands off for a second and we of our own will then take our little feet to where things begin to go against us. Then we begin to cry out but He knows that it is the right field where He can do the most work in us. Yes, He will allow us to get into a bind so that He can begin to do His work in our lives.

He led the children of Israel through the wilderness for the purpose that Moses outlined and we are not different from the children of Israel in His dealing with us. Moses said that "He might humble you and that He might prove you." You know how it feels when we come to church and we are feeling very good and loving towards the Lord and we are dancing around, and we make all these promises to Him about how our lives now belong to Him. We tell Him how we want Him to conform us to the image of His Son and how we will do anything He wants us to do and we are serious about it. When we go home, some of us forget our "feeling good promises and vows" to the Lord but the Lord does not forget them. One day, He decides it is time for Him to collect on those promises and vows and He begins to work in our lives to accomplish what we asked Him to do in us and we begin to feel the flame of His fire as He puts us on the Potter's Wheel to mold us!

God wants to Know How Deep Your Love Is:

I usually talk about His arm but He also has a very powerful finger and I believe that He looks into your life and identifies the one thing that is most important to you and He puts His powerful finger right on top of that thing. Because we are not aware of His powerful finger, we go around praying, singing, dancing and decreeing and we seem to be living on cloud nine because whenever we ask the Lord for something, our prayers and our requests are immediately answered. Then, one day, we decide to ask for this one thing that is most important to us; we will pray, decree, remind God of His promises, fast and pray some more but nothing happens.

You know what I am talking about; that thing that you have

prayed about everyday, that you have cried about and that you got angry at God about. We call our friends to agree with us in prayer but still nothing happens. We then go to our churches and we put in a prayer request but nothing happens and because our pastors love us, they send out an email or tell the church intercessors to pray for the need but nothing happens. We hear that there is a conference in town and the minister works miracles, he has raised people from the dead and when he prays for people they get breakthrough and so we run over there and pay a hundred dollars to get into the conference and when we come back, still nothing happens. The reason nothing happens is because God has put His finger on it in your life because He knows it will get the most of your attention.

For a lot of men and women, it is marriage, having a child, finances, promotion, a new home, a new car, etc. As I said, He knows exactly what it is in your life that He needs to He put His finger right on and He has you where He wants you—on your kneels! Why does He do this? Because, He has to prove you and if for nothing else, you will learn how to pray earnestly. He proves your love for Him. Remember the song that goes, *"How deep is your love? Is your love found deep? I really need to know?"* Yes, He will come and prove this in your life and He will give you a chance to prove your promises that you made to Him to see if you were really serious. He wants to know: Would you really love Me when things are not going your way? Would you really love Me when everybody is against you? Will I still be your number one if you cannot pay your rent?

Meanwhile, He is very much in your life and He sees you cry, quote all the scriptures and also lash out at Him and He is right there. If you are one who sees into the spirit realm, you will sometimes see Him carrying you and rocking you just like a Father does a crying child and you might think why don't You just pay the bill, give me a spouse, give me the finances, etc. He does not immediately provide you with these things because He wants you to go through the process so that He can transform you and at the end, do you good.

Learning God's Priority:

Just as you are not supposed to live by bread alone but by every Word that God has spoken, you are also not to seek other things first but the kingdom of God in your life. When you have mastered the kingdom principles, then He can begin to manifest the kingdom blessings in your life because you can handle the blessings properly because you have mastered the kingdom principles:

> "<u>For after all these things do the Gentiles seek</u>: for your heavenly Father knoweth that ye have need of all these things. *33* <u>But seek ye first the kingdom of God</u>, and <u>his righteousness</u>; and <u>all these things shall be added unto you</u>" (Matthew 6: 32-33).

You can see that the pursuit of kingdom, kingdom principles and righteousness are to take precedence over our personal needs and desires. This is a very hard and painful lesson to learn when you first begin to walk with God.

For some people, this process can last twenty years because they do not get to know why they are going through the things that the Lord allows them to go through and they become resentful and are bitter towards Him and His church. Again, I say to you that God will come into your life to prove you when you come into the kingdom but you decide how long the process will take by your reactions to the tests. Because the children of Israel murmured and complained, their processing took forty years! We see this restated in **Exodus 20:20:**

> "And Moses said unto the people, Fear not: <u>for God is come to prove you</u>, and <u>that his fear may be before your faces, that ye sin not</u>."

How many of you believe that God comes to prove you? God cares so much more about you making it into heaven than He does about you getting one thousand dollars to pay your bill. There are some people who are believing the Lord for millions of dollars worth of contracts and I tell some of them that if God gave it to them, they will drop out of church because they will become too busy in their business to have time for God. Therefore, God comes and He proves you and He makes sure that He lays a foundation in you that can sustain the structures that He wants in your life. He makes sure that you know His priorities as well as His ways. Jesus said it, that when a man wants to build a house, he will first have to make sure that he counts the costs before he begins to build. It is the same way with God because He comes to prove you to see how much He can really build in your life. He sees that you come to church and you are the first to lie flat on the ground to demonstrate your love for Him publicly but He wants to try you privately to see if you will still be standing when the rubber meets the road in your life.

He also wants to plug up the leaking parts of your life that will not be able to sustain His blessings. I told you in Chapter 2 of this book (under the subheading, *Divine Provision*) that God showed me a vision of all the prayers that I have prayed to Him and all the prayers that I will ever pray in my lifetime. He arranged them on His board according to His order of priority. At the top of them was **knowledge** and when He went to the board to put a checkmark on the one that He was granting me, He did not look at the rest of my request. He checked off knowledge because He said that I was too ignorant of His ways to be able to walk in what I was asking for! He also informed me that part of the blessings being manifested in my life today were the answers to the prayers that my dad had prayed but could not walk in because he did not understand spiritual warfare! Do you now see why knowing Him and His ways are a must? Ignorance can delay the manifestations of your blessings.

The Importance of the Fear of the Lord:

The one time Jesus ever told us to fear was when He said in **Luke 12:5, "But I will forewarn you whom ye shall fear: Fear him, which after he hath killed hath power to cast into hell; yea,**

I say unto you, Fear him." If God gives you everything you want from Him without the fear of the Lord in you, you might end up in hell because many of us are sitting here today and the only thing that is keeping us from doing all the lofty things that we want to do and all the grandeur things that we want to do is lack of finances. If God gave each and everyone of us twenty million dollars a piece right now, you will see who we really are, you will see if our humility is really genuine and if our love for God lasts.

My younger brother believes that money changes people and I do believe that without a solid foundation and without the fear of the Lord, money truly will alter the character and behavior of some people. Think about it; when you no longer have to call anybody to do anything for you, you have the finances to indulge yourself in your heart's desires and no one can tell you what you can or cannot do, then the real you will come out. This is why God proves us in order to show us what is not of Him that is in us that we might not know or that we refuse to acknowledge.

When you have all the finances that you need and all the influence that you desire, you also need to have enough of the fear of God to keep you from indulging yourself in things that might defile, dishonor and damn your soul. This is why the Bible tells us in **Proverbs 9:10** that:

"The fear of the LORD is the beginning of wisdom: and the knowledge of the holy is understanding."

Having a good understanding of this scripture above and applying it in our lives will determine how far each and every one of us would go with the Lord. Although you love and reverence God, you must also fear God enough to stay away from acts of sin. God hates sin and according to Him, **"The soul that sinneth, it shall die"** (Ezekiel 18:20). You cannot continue to live a life of sin after receiving the Lord Jesus as your Savior and expect God to condone your actions. This is why God chastens us to the point that it does not matter what we have or where we are because we are committed to a love of righteousness and have a perfect hatred for evil.

God does not condone disobedience nor does He allow people to work contrary to His Word and not do something about it. He said in **Leviticus 26:23-25** that He will punish those who do not want him to reform them. His desire is to reform us by conforming us to His ways with His Word. Therefore, we all need to embrace His crucible and willingly submit to His Potter's Wheel.

> "**And if ye will not be reformed by me by these things, but will walk contrary unto me;** *24* **Then will I also walk contrary unto you, and will punish you yet seven times for your sins.** *25* And I will bring a sword upon you, that shall avenge the quarrel of my covenant: and when ye are gathered together within your cities, I will send the pestilence among you; and ye shall be delivered into the hand of the enemy."

Sometimes you talk about scriptures or events that are in the Old Testament and some people have to see them in the New Testament for them to register in their mind. Therefore, we are now going to look at the New Testament to see how God deals with the new believer. The children of Israel were chastened by their wilderness experience and we are told in **Hebrews 12:5-8** that God also chastens every new believer:

> "And ye have forgotten the exhortation which speaketh unto you as unto children, **My son, despise not thou the chastening of the Lord, nor faint when thou art rebuked of him**: *6* **For whom the Lord loveth he chasteneth, and scourgeth every son whom he receiveth.** *7* **If ye endure chastening, God dealeth with you as with sons**; for what son is he whom the father chasteneth not? *8* **But if ye be without chastisement, whereof all are partakers, then are ye bastards, and not sons.**"

God chastens us because He desires for us to be a clean, holy and righteous; people whom given any circumstances will always hate evil and choose righteousness. Again I say to you that God will allow you to be tried so that He can let you see what is in your heart. If it is love, greed, evil, etc., it will come out. For example, as a newly born again Christian, some former friends of yours might come to your house and say to you, "We can tell you this because we trust you and we know that you are our friend. We went and robbed an establishment last night and we took twenty million dollars but we know that you are a good person so out of the twenty million dollars we want to give you two million dollars if you will just bless us and help us hide the money in your house." That old devil will immediately tell you to bless and help them; after all, you are not the one that stole the money and God said, "Bless everybody."

Yes, he will give you a scripture to manipulate you so that you can feel safe to become a partaker of the robbery. But when God has laid a solid foundation in you, it will not be difficult for you to choose righteousness over evil. You will fear God enough that even behind closed doors, you will choose that which is right and godly and would bring Him glory with your life.

So **Hebrews 12:6** tells us that when God receives us into His kingdom, there must be a chastening and a scourging in our lives. This process is not just reserved for some but for all. In other words, if God does not love you enough to chasten you and set you on the right path, then you are not really a child of God. He loves us so much that when we come to Him, He beats the foolishness out of us. As I stated before, seven months after I became born again, I had a divine visitation from God and the devil also showed up after He left. A few days later, I ended up in a psychiatric hospital because I was seeing the good, the bad and the ugly spirits and I felt as if my life had been turned upside down! A very powerful spirit of discernment was given to me and because of it I could see the evil spirits in a person. I could be talking to someone and the evil spirits in the person would just flash me with their presence in the person and I would watch as the spirits freely move about in the person.

I had no prior training about what to do because I had become "a free thinker" and an agnostic because of my philosophy classes in school. I immediately got cured of my agnosticism and free thinking but I could not make the evil spirits go away from around me and from the people that I meet on a daily basis. I remember asking the Lord if I did wrong by coming to Him and becoming born again. It was as if all hell broke loose in my life as the devil and his evil spirits were making their daily tormenting and harassing appearances in my life. My life became like a nightmare and I wanted help to deal with what was going on.

True to His Word, God delivered me and anointed me to drive out evil spirits. I learned to pray, I learned spiritual warfare, and I learned the power of the Word of God. I saw first hand the faithfulness of God to move on our behalf when we call but what I could not understand was why He would allow me to go through this major crisis when He loves me so much. I was baffled by His actions and when I asked Him about it He said, "I was looking for the right soil for my seed." According to Him He had to plow the soil of my heart with the events so that He could remove the things that could choke His seed in me. Also, I heard a teaching by a Prophet named Graham Cooke and he talked about how God processes us His children when we first come to Him. He talked about how that God will take you and He will lock you up in a dark room. In there, He will beat the hell and foolishness out of you till you can barely stand and then He goes, "Now you are ready." As I stated before, many of us are strong in our own strength but God does not need our strength. He will deal with you until you are ready to loose your own strength, opinion and your "zeal without knowledge" and place your trust in Him. You must be willing to lay down your own will and do His will. This is hard for all of us. Even the Lord Jesus sweated blood in His efforts to lay down His will and go to the Cross in obedience to the Father's will.

As I said, what got me into trouble more so than anything else was my "zeal without knowledge." I see things spiritually on people and about people and I used to just rush out there and talk to them without even consulting the Lord first. Some Christians can be cruel; especially if they believe that a Christian cannot have a demon. They will say some things to you that will make you run to the Lord in tears. I used to just get in trouble spiritually with the Lord, with the devil and in the physical with God's children. One day, I went to the Lord and I said, "I am tired of being beaten up by You, the devil and Your children. What do I do in order not to get beat up? How do I walk this walk in a safe way?" He winked as He said to me, "There is a path that the ravenous bird has not seen" and I said, "You mean there is a place where the devil is blind?" I knew that I needed to find this place so I said, "Where is this path?" He led me to **Job 28:7-8:**

> "**There is a path which no fowl knoweth, and which the vulture's eye hath not seen:** *8* **The lion's whelps have not trodden it, nor the fierce lion passed by it.**" (KJV)

Other translations read as follow:

> "**No bird of prey knows that hidden path, no falcon's eye has seen it.** *8* **Proud beasts do not set foot on it, and no lion prowls there**" (NIV).

> "**Vultures are blind to its riches, hawks never lay eyes on it.** *8* **Wild animals are oblivious to it, lions don't know it's there**" (The Message).

Yes, there is a path of safety in the Lord and when you are on it you are dwelling in the secret place where the devil cannot make you suffer damages as before. You will learn how not to let him monitor your activities. When God begins to lead you in this path, it does not mean that the devil will no longer be coming against you but it means that you are no longer going to be taking his hits and getting knocked down. You are no longer going to be one who is overwhelmed by your circumstances because wisdom begins to give you an explanation as to what is going on, why they are going on and what you should do to walk in victory.

As this begins to happen, you then realize that you are going through the process with God and it is for a good purpose. He told me not to murmur and complain when things that I do not like are happening but instead to stop and ask Him to help me understand why they are happening and for what purpose. When I began to do this, I realized that He would most times allow some of the things just as He did Job because He wants to give me an anointing and a level of wisdom that will help me and other people! I no longer complain about His process even when they feel hard and cruel. My trials have also become shorter because I no longer prolong them by complaining. We are to be like Jesus who for the joy and glory that was set before Him endured the shame of the Cross. We should always rejoice because we are going to come out on the other side with a new anointing.

When you understand this, it makes your trials easier and it makes your expectation in the Lord and your faith stronger. This is why the above scripture says that there is a path which no foul knoweth. Who are the fouls and the vultures? They are the devil and his demons. As you learn to walk closely with Wisdom and to obey her instructions, the vultures and the fouls will not be able to locate you or your godly activities to hinder or destroy them. **This means that after you have learned not to make covenants with the devil and his agents, after you have learned to remove his legalities and technicalities against you, after you have learned to watch your words and make sure that your doctrines and your beliefs are right, there is a way that you can walk in which the devil will be blind in your life because you are actually walking under the shadow of the Almighty.** When He revealed this to me, I said to Him, this is the path that I want You to lead me in. When you are on this path, you understand the purposes of trials and you know the benefits in each trial for you and you can actually rejoice as you watch the foolishness of the devil.

The path of safety continues in **Psalm 32:7-8:**

"Thou art my hiding place; thou shalt preserve

me from trouble; thou shalt compass me about with songs of deliverance. Selah. *8* **I will instruct thee and teach thee in the way which thou shalt go: I will guide thee with mine eye.**"

The Lord's promise to those on the path of safety is to guide them closely with His eye. Wisdom is promising that when you get to this path (a safe place in God), i.e., when you come to an understanding of the ways of the Lord, God Himself leads you very closely on a daily basis. When I talk about getting to the path, I am not talking about how long you have been born again because some people can be born again for twenty, forty years and they do not know anything about the ways of the Lord; all they still know are the acts of the Lord and they judge Him, they complain and they murmur when things do not go their way.

When the Lord began to teach me about this path, He took me to a scripture in Job and He showed me how the devil made a proposition about humanity in **Job 1:9-11.** The devil had visited Job with his evil intentions prior to this conversation with God but he discovered that Job and his possessions were protected by God and so he was powerless against Job. He believed that Job was only serving God because of what he gets from God. The devil's proposition is that Job (man) is basically a very selfish being that watches out only for himself and he (man) serves God just because of what he gets from God:

> "Then Satan answered the LORD, and said, **Doth Job fear** *(by serving or doing His will)* **God for nought?** *10* **Hast not thou made an hedge about him,** and **about his house,** and **about all that he hath on every side? thou hast blessed the work of his hands,** and **his substance is increased in the land.** *11* **But put forth thine hand now, and touch all that he hath,** and **he will curse thee to thy face.**"

As you can see from this scripture above, Job was walking with God in safety and protection prior to his trials. It was not until God gave the devil permission that the devil could touch Job and his possessions. Job was actually in God's path of safety. The Lord gave the devil permission to prove Job's integrity (love for God) and the devil went and he destroyed all of Job's possessions including his children but Job never spoke an evil word against God! Therefore, God said to the devil, have you seen that Job kept his integrity and has not spoken against me but the devil replied, yes, he has not but I tell you what, a man will give everything that he has for his skin and his life. In other words, a man will give all that he has to save his life. Therefore, he said to God, You just touch Job's flesh and touch his skin and see if he will not curse You to Your face.

> **"And Satan answered the LORD, and said, <u>Skin for skin, yea, all that a man hath will he give for his life</u>. 5 But put forth thine hand now, and touch his bone and his flesh, and he will curse thee to thy face"** (Job 2:4-5).

What the devil is saying is that we are basically a selfish people but Job proved him wrong because even at the end, Job did not sin with his lips by speaking against God. Look at what Job said in **Job 2:10** when the devil inspired his wife to tell him to curse God:

> **"But he said unto her, <u>Thou speakest as one of the foolish women speaketh</u>. What? shall we receive good at the hand of God, and shall we not receive evil? <u>In all this did not Job sin with his lips</u>."**

The core of Job's test was, how faithful will he be to God when he losses all that he has and his life is in the balance? Job proved his love for God by not charging God foolishly. He disproved the devil's theory that we are serving God because of what He gives us.

Also, God the Father showed me how that the Lord Jesus also disproved the devil's theory that man is a selfish being who will give anything to save his life because the Lord laid down His life for us! He said, "Look at what My Son did." The Lord Jesus told us in **John 15:13** that, **"Greater love has no man than this, that a man would come and lay down his life for his friends."** He disproved what the devil said to God, that we are serving Him for selfish reasons and that we are going to curse God with our lips if we do not get what we want from Him.

According to devil, we are our own number one and we watch out only for number one but Jesus came and did the exact opposite —He laid down His own life for us all. **At the end, God the Father said to me that the trials, the difficult circumstances and the adverse conditions that the devil sends against us are tests which allow us to show why we are serving God, how deep our love is and how faithful we are to God**. If each one of us is pressed long enough or deep enough, what is going to come out of us? When the devil starts to squeeze you, do you blame God or charge Him foolishly with your mouth? If you do, you cannot remain on the path of safety because you make yourself vulnerable to the devil.

When you gain the understanding that you are in this walk with the Lord till the end and you begin to let Him guide you, you will stop insisting on your own opinion or your own will. You now trust that God knows what is best for you. I told you in Chapter 2 of this book (under the subheading: *Bond Slave Covenant*) that I made a request to be His bond slave. It was the best thing that I ever did for myself. After He taught me about the ground rules of being a slave; meaning that a slave has no rights and no opinions, He said to me as long as someone is living and eating from the "tree of the knowledge of good and evil," the person will always have a reason to say that God has been unfair. According to Him, because the person's sense of what is right and wrong will be so high that the person will judge God by his or her standards. When God is doing something that the person does not understand, the person will judge God as being unjust or unfair. This type of person cannot remain on the path of safety.

A case in point is the Cross. The disciples did not understand why the Lord who did so many good things for others and who healed and raised people from the dead would just die on the Cross without God's intervention. It was not until the Lord rose again that He began to open their understanding to the "hidden work and wisdom" that God displayed by allowing His Son to die the way He did! Therefore, we cannot insist on our own sense of right and wrong about situations but we must be willing to lay it down and eat only from the tree of Life. This means that we have to be led by the Holy Spirit and obey the instructions that He gives us at the expense of our own opinion. One of the first things that the Lord said to me after my being born again was, "If you want to be successful in walking with Me, you must do what I did; lay down your own will and say 'not my will but Your will be done.'" I say to Him all the time that I know nothing by myself, I understand nothing by myself and I can do nothing by myself. Therefore, as He commands me, so will I do all the days of my life. God's ways are very different from ours so we must always trust that He is working all thongs for our good.

At this stage of your Christian walk, you must learn to rely on the Holy Spirit more so than you ever did before and you must learn to go to Him about every single thing that you want to do. When you do this, you place yourself in a position where God lets you know when you are about to do something that He is not involved in or that He does not want you to do. When you get His OK on a project, you have the confidence that He will back you up. This is how He showed me the value of **Romans 8:14** that says:

"For <u>as many as are led by the Spirit of God, they are the sons of God</u>."

We must be led by the Holy Spirit in all that we do. As I said before, iniquity is doing your own thing in your own way but we must all learn to do what God wants us to do and not what we want to do. Jesus relied on the Holy Spirit for everything that He said and did. He said in **John 8:28:**

> "Then said Jesus unto them, When ye have lifted up the Son of man, then shall ye know that I am he, <u>and that I do nothing of myself</u>; <u>but as my Father hath taught me, I speak these things</u>."

This means that you must come to the place where God begins to instruct you "line upon line and precept upon precept." This was the stage at which He said to me, "I want you to ask Me to teach you how to ask Me questions." So, if I do not understand something, before I put my two cents in, I say to the Lord, "Lord, what is Your opinion about this thing?"

He said to me, "Another reason you need to learn to ask Me questions is because, you can easily become the biggest persecutor of the new move of My Spirit when you see something that I am doing that is new to you and you do not come to Me to ask for understanding." Therefore, we cannot just say away with something that we do not understand because, it might be something that God is doing. Being totally dependent on the Holy Spirit helps us to avoid this. It helps us to stay on the path of safety. It is why the Bible admonishes us in **Proverbs 3:5** as follows:

> "Trust in the LORD with all thine heart; and lean not unto thine own understanding."

As you begin to walk in this path of safety, you will find that God sends His Angel to go with you in this path. Remember what He said to Moses in the wilderness? He said in **Exodus 23:20-21:**

> "Behold, <u>I send an Angel before thee, to keep thee in the way</u>, and <u>to bring thee into the place which I have prepared</u>. *21* Beware of him, and obey his voice, provoke him not; for he will not pardon your transgressions: for my name is in him."

When you are being led by the Holy Spirit, you find out that you have an understanding into the ways of the Lord that transcends the understanding most of the people around you. As I said before, when you are going through difficult times, you now know how to stop and ask the for the purpose of the test. You are also confident that you will come out of it victorious.

As for me, I can now rest in the Lord because I know that when I go to a place and the spirits there come against me, God is actually giving me an opportunity to receive a new anointing and it has changed my attitude about spiritual warfare. It is exciting to receive different anointings against different spirits and for different tasks: Therefore, I am constantly asking the Lord for the anointing to minister in new environments so that I can destroy the uncircumcised Philistines that have been holding the people bound in these places. I am no longer afraid to go places or to be in the battlefront.

We are all given righteousness as a gift when we come into God's kingdom but our works here on earth will be tried in heaven by God's fire of love. Only the works done in love will stand and the works that were based on other motives will burn up in the fire of love. The level of our productivity (the sum of your work) is going to determine the sphere of influence that we receive from the Lord at the end. Therefore, we want to be on this path of safety so that we can bring many into God's kingdom and have our needs met by Him and not suffer loss from the enemy and we want our works to be much at the end. As a result, each one of us needs to ask, who am I influencing for the Lord today? What am I doing for God today? Who am I turning back from going to hell today for the Lord? A lot of us are going to stand before the Lord and will see tears in His eyes as He says, "I gave you My Son and I gave you My Holy Spirit and you could not even tell one person about Me to turn the person from hell to Me? You did not love Me enough to make a difference in the life of another person for Me?"

On one *Father's Day*, I was feeling happy and I said to the Lord, "Father, I want to bless You on this Father's Day and I want to do something special for You. What do You want?" He said to me, "Bring me more children; go out there and evangelize to win souls for Me." He loves the world and He wants the lost souls saved and we should be willing to pay the price so that we can give Him His heart's desire. A lot of people are still bound in pagan religions and it is God's heart cry that none of them should perish. Have you stopped to think about the billions of people that are currently held in bondage by the spirits of Islam, Buddhism, Hinduism, etc.? We have to position ourselves to receive knowledge, wisdom and understanding on how to win these souls for the Lord and we want to walk in God's path of safety while we are doing it.

Psalm 91 also speaks about the path of safety:

> "**He that dwelleth in the secret place of the most High shall abide under the shadow of the Almighty.** *2* I will say of the LORD, **He is my refuge and my fortress**: my God; **in him will I trust**. *3* **Surely he shall deliver thee from the snare of the fowler, and from the noisome pestilence.** *4* **He shall cover thee with his feathers**, and **under his wings shalt thou trust: his truth shall be thy shield and buckler.** *5* **Thou shalt not be afraid for the terror by night; nor for the arrow that flieth by day;** *6* **Nor for the pestilence that walketh in darkness; nor for the destruction that wasteth at noonday.** *7* A thousand shall fall at thy side, and ten thousand at thy right hand; but it shall not come nigh thee. *8* **Only with thine eyes shalt thou behold and see the reward of the wicked.** *9* **Because thou hast made the LORD, which is my refuge, even the most High, thy habitation;** *10* **There shall no evil befall thee, neither shall any plague come nigh thy dwelling.** *11* **For he shall give his angels charge over thee, to keep thee in all thy ways.** *12* They shall bear thee up in their hands, lest thou dash thy foot against a stone. **the young lion and the dragon shalt thou trample under feet.** *13* **Thou shalt tread upon the lion and adder:**"

In this secret place, you find that God is actually the one that over shadows you. This is why the vulture's eye cannot see you in this path. Evil shall not befall you in this path and no plague shall come near your dwelling. You are completely shielded by the Almighty.

You are able to tread down the devil's plans against you because the Lord shows them to you beforehand. Once He gave me a vision of what He is talking about in Psalm 91. In this vision, I saw Him sitting on His throne and I was a little child sitting between His legs playing while He watched over me just like other fathers would watch their little kids playing.

I came away thinking, who in the world is going to come against me and win when I am in between the legs of God Almighty? Who can come between the legs of the Lord when He is the one surrounding me? The answer is nobody. I am not the only one that can sit between His legs because God is no respecter of person. We all get from God what we have enough time, devotion and willingness to receive from Him. We have to learn how not to be presumptuous in our walk with the Lord but instead find out what He wants done and how He wants it done. We cannot be led by our good intentions and say, "I knew that it was the right thing to do so I went ahead and did it" without consulting the Lord. When God visits your works or when you get into trouble spiritually, He will then ask you, "Did I tell you to do it?"

I was one of those people that knew exactly what they wanted to do for the Lord without consulting Him. I left New York and I decided that I was going to spend my life doing good deeds for God and I would seek out people that needed help and I would go out there and do whatever it was they needed help doing. I just made myself available to people and I did not mind the fact that it did not bring me any money. Therefore, if God was telling me not to do anything, I could not hear Him because I was too busy doing the good deeds for Him and relying on myself. One day, His Almighty Finger located my finances and He said to me, "I want you to empty your bank account and put it all in the offering basket" and I was like, "What?" He said, "You heard Me, empty your bank account and put the money in the offering basket." He definitely got my attention.

Have your knees ever gone weak and buckled when you hear something? I was shaken by His request but I knew it was Him telling me to do it so I knew that I had to obey Him. Because of this request, I thought that God absolutely hated me but I went and empted my bank account and put the money in the offering basket. After that, He said to me, when you were in New York, you had a savings account that you purposely put money in as your back up account for emergency needs. I wrote to the bank and withdrew the money in that account also and I put the check in the offering basket. I also had some stocks and CDs left that I had not cashed out and I went ahead and cashed them out and put the money in the offering basket. I did it all grudgingly and I was left with nothing. I was keenly aware of my position financially and I knew then that I had to depend on God to help me financially and in every area of my life. It was the beginning of my wilderness journey.

It was all new to me because as long as I had money to do things for people and buy things for people, I felt like a very good person and I did not stop to consult Him concerning the things that I was doing. He knew what the problem was and He knew what would get rid of it and He got my attention. Do you know that after I obeyed Him and had no more money to support me while I went around doing my "good deeds" that I could hear Him clearly? I mean, I could now hear His instructions because I was holding on to Him for my dear life. I could hear Him say to me, do this and do not do that, whereas before I could not hear because I was too busy doing things for Him.

Before this time, it never occurred to me that God might be dealing with some people through their circumstances but I had appointed myself as their deliverer and was actually not allowing God to work in their lives as they continue to look up to me. I was shocked to discover that God was not in most of the things that I spent my days (two years) doing for Him. This is why God processes us so that we do not use our financial resources to hinder His purposes in people's lives. It pays to be lead by the Holy Spirit.

Understanding the Need for Holiness:

Walking in holiness will help you to stay on the part of safety. How many of you know that the scriptures tell us that without holiness no man shall see God? **The two things that will make you to see God quickly in your life are holiness and a pure heart.** If you want to see God move in your circumstance, your situation and in your life on a daily basis, just purpose that you are going to walk in holiness and that your heart is going to be pure concerning people. As you learn to turn the other cheek, God will then become your defender. For instance, if someone says something ugly to you, God will rise up to defend you even when you are not aware of what they said or did to you that was ungodly.

Sometimes God will let something happen to you to perfect your walk in holiness. A case in point was a recent incident in my own life that involved my taking a very bad fall. I did not break any bones or fractured anything but the fall was bad because I found myself falling backward and I tried hard to break the fall but I landed on my fanny and it hurt. I was surprised that the Lord allowed me to take such a bad fall without picking me up or warning me about it because He does not allow bad things to surprise me. He usually forewarns me so I actually got a little angry at Him because I knew that there could have been an angel to help me break the fall. Therefore, I asked Him why He did not help me or forewarn me about the fall. First, He let me see that He allowed me to fall on the part of my body that could protect me from breaking or fracturing any bone. Then, He said to me, "Did I not say, touch not mine anointed and do my prophets no harm? I know the scripture says this in **Psalm 105:15:**

"Saying, <u>Touch not mine anointed, and do my prophets no harm</u>."

Also in **Isaiah 54:15:**

"Behold, they shall surely gather together, but not by me: <u>whosoever shall gather together against</u>

<u>**thee shall fall for thy sake.**</u>"

In **Proverbs 28:18:**

"**Whoso walketh uprightly shall be saved: <u>but he that is perverse in his ways shall fall at once</u>.**"

I knew immediately that my fall was a judgment for something that had I said or done to one of His children. I wanted to know what I did and He said, "You rose up against your sister and you are a partaker of the grace that is upon her because she prayed you into the kingdom. Just because you are older than her, you rose up against her and you had to fall because the scripture over her is, 'whosoever shall rise up against her shall fall.'" He was right because earlier that day, I had called up my youngest sister in Nigeria to vent my anger on her because I was taking care of some government matter for our mother and I wanted her to handle it because she is an attorney. Rather than take care of the matter, she sent my mother's driver to take care of it and of course, it was not done properly. I was very angry when I found out what happened and because she is my youngest sister, I totally disregarded the fact that she is also a pastor and I began to sound off on her about how she needed to be a more involved in her legal profession. I took the fall a few hours later! I had to repent for not validating her as a pastor, for judging her because she was not fully involved in her legal profession and for coming down hard on her because she did not do what I had requested.

To remain on the path of safety, I learned that I had to lay off God's children even when they are my immediate relatives. I was judged because my sister is on that path of safety in her choices but I had put my two cents into it contrary to God's will. When you are in the path of safety, God becomes an enemy to your enemies and He contends with them that contend with you. My sister in not my enemy but I had touched her with my tongue so I took the fall.

"<u>**For I will contend with him that contendeth with thee**</u>**, and I will save thy children**" (Isaiah 49: 25).

> "**Since thou wast precious in my sight, thou hast been honourable**, and I have loved thee: **therefore will I give men for thee, and people for thy life**" (Isaiah 43:4).

I learned that even when walking closely with the Lord, you have to be careful not to take certain liberties for yourself and begin to do things that will bring His judgment against you. A life of holiness is a must for all those that desire to walk closely with the Lord. No matter how close you are to the Lord, He will judge you when you walk in iniquity rather than holiness. When we walk in iniquity even for a day, we step away from His path of safety into the enemy's territory. His grace usually leads us to repentance so living a life of holiness should be our daily commitment. David who was "a man after God's heart" got judged by God in **2 Samuel 12:9-10** when he killed Uriah for his wife Bathsheba. God told him that because he killed Uriah with a sword, the sword will never depart from his house:

> **"Wherefore hast thou despised the commandment of the LORD, to do evil in his sight? thou hast killed Uriah the Hittite with the sword, and hast taken his wife to be thy wife, and hast slain him with the sword of the children of Ammon. *10* Now therefore the sword shall never depart from thine house; because thou hast despised me, and hast taken the wife of Uriah the Hittite to be thy wife."**

God forgave David's sin when he repented but the judgment was manifested in his children; especially in Absalom. To remain in the path of safety, we must forsake iniquities and pursue a life of holiness and integrity.

The Highway of Safety:

Let us take a look at **Isaiah 35:8-10** which also talks about this path of safety. The prophet Isaiah called it "an highway" and "the way of holiness." It reads:

> "And **an highway shall be there, and a way, and it shall be called The way of holiness; the unclean shall not pass over it**; but it shall be for those: the wayfaring men, though fools, shall not err therein. *9* **No lion shall be there, nor any ravenous beast shall go up thereon, it shall not be found there; but the redeemed shall walk there:** *10* And the ransomed of the LORD shall return, and come to Zion with songs and everlasting joy upon their heads: **they shall obtain joy and gladness, and sorrow and sighing shall flee away**."

This means that if you do not purpose to put your life in God's will and ways, you are not a candidate to be on this path of safety. As you can see from the above scripture, those who live contrary to God's Word, who live a life of sin, who are involved in things that defile the soul and body (unclean), etc., are not allowed to enter this path of safety. As long as you have one foot in the world and one foot in the church, you can forget about being on this path or highway. As I said before, God has a safe place just like He told Moses in **Exodus 33:21-22** that there is a place by Him where Moses can be hidden in the cleft of the Rock.

> "And the LORD said, **Behold, there is a place by me, and thou shalt stand upon a rock:** *22* And it shall come to pass, while my glory passeth by, that **I will put thee in a clift of the rock**, and will cover thee with my hand while I pass by…"

There is a place by God where we can walk in safety and God said that while we are in this place, our enemies will be at peace with us because God becomes our defender. I have learned not to defend myself anymore but to leave my defense to the Lord when I am dealing with unkind people. When somebody says something ugly or unkind to me and I know that I have not provoked or wrong the person, I just call on the Lord. On the other hand, except for the times that some people just got on my last nerve (let's get honest),

I am usually quick to apologize when I am wrong or have done something a person does not like. I am quick to say that I am sorry when I am wrong but when people persecute me for no reason, God will be the one to judge them. When you purpose to stay on this path of safety, you will discover that God always forewarns you when something evil is about to happen so that you can speak His Word to prevent it from happening.

Seven Privileges of Being On the Path of Safety:

Being on the path of safety has many benefits and privileges that we need to appropriate for ourselves. Let us look at some of them.

1. God's Friend and Confidant:
You become God's friend and God's confidant when you walk with Him on the path of safety or in the secret path. As His friend, God begins to confide in you some of His plans, secrets, ways, etc. As I sated before, Elisha and God had so close a relationship that God could confide in him on a daily basis. One day, God the Father asked me to be His confidant and I said yes. Not long after that, He woke me up one night and said in a whisper, "I have superstars in My house you know" and I said, "Really?" He continued, "They come into My sanctuary as superstars after praise and worship is over; is praise and worship not supposed to be about Me?" I said yes, praise and worship is about Him and in honor of Him. Still speaking in a whisper He said, "They do everything as superstars in my house except sign autographs! They are ushered in and out and they do not interact with My children but My Son, Jesus went among the people and they were able to touch Him and get healed." He continued still in a whisper, "You know what else? They want Me to give them My power. What do you think that they would do with it?" Then, He thundered as He declared, "But, I will not give it to them." As you can see from this encounter, you do come to a place in your walk with the Lord that you are not only safe but you are His friend and confidant. He confides in you about what He likes and what He does not like and how you can avoid the pitfalls that others have already fallen into.

He spoke those things to me so that I could learn from the mistakes of those who view themselves as superstars because God has given them a national and international platform to speak from. He said to me, "When you go out there, I want you to keep it simple." I have since come to realize that it is not as complicated as some of God's "superstars" would have us to believe because it is all by His grace. If you begin to think of yourself as a superstar, God would let you stumble so that you can learn that it is His grace that sustains you on a daily basis. For example, not too long ago, I was in a conference in which one of God's "superstars" was the guest minister and of course, before getting on the pulpit, he went on and on about himself and with a lot of pomp and we all watched him. Do you know that when he got to the pulpit, he forgot his message and we all waited for almost five minutes because he could not remember his sermon! He had no clue what he was supposed to minister on and everybody stared in amazement. I believe that God has a way of dealing with those who become legends in their own minds.

The Lord also told me that He has set revolving doors in some of the churches because they think when He said to go win souls that He told them go fill their churches with members. He said, "The more people they bring in, the more He allows the ones that were there before to leave." So, it is like an endless cycle; therefore some leave and some come. According to Him, Jesus went out there and preached the Gospel and He was never particular about the church building or filling a particular church with members as some pastors now do. Having a large number of members and not truly transforming lives is now the goal of most churches. Therefore, the Lord said to me, when you go out there and sow my Word into the lives of people, I will bring the people that you need in your church. It is true that when you give to the poor, you lend to the Lord and He alone can determine how to pay you back.

We must aggressively pursue soul winning. **It grieves me to hear the new fancy preaching in the church today in which God's own ministers are preaching that evangelism and soul winning are not God's primary agenda but setting up businesses**

for workplace ministry, getting connected with leaders of nations for prosperity and winning over the ten percent wealthiest and most influential members of nations is what God's agenda is all about. According to them, winning this group is the key to possessing the nations. **They down play evangelism while they preach the "Wall Street Gospel" but they are all wrong because soul winning is the foundation on which everything else is built. We need to reach all members of every society every where because the Lord Jesus came to win the souls of men.** Therefore, I say to all who read this book that soul winning must come first because it is about souls going to heaven and not hell. The Lord asked in **Mark 8:36,** "What will it profit a man to gain the whole world and lose his soul?"

As God's confidant, when something strange is happening to you and you ask Him about it, wisdom will speak to you. Wisdom is always speaking to those that would listen. When you look at the book of Proverbs, you will see that Wisdom is a speaker and that She speaks all the time. Day and night She is speaking as She calls out to people in the highways and in the byways and Her message is for those who are simple to come to Her and get some wisdom because wisdom is better than silver and gold. Wisdom is always speaking but we have to learn how to come into that place where we position ourselves for God's divine wisdom to begin to lead us. This means that we are willing to die to our flesh and our sense of right and wrong so that Truth (the Word of God) can determine the outcome of what we do.

2. You Will Receive the Ability to Discern God's Voice:

There are times that we pray and expect God to manifest the answer the way that He normally does but there are times that the Lord will position us in such a way that we have to do an act of kindness or love for someone else in order for us to receive what we asked for. It is one of God's tests and only walking close to Him in His divine wisdom and as His confidant can we discern what we are required to do or what is going on concerning our situation or prayers. God does not like to be put in a box by anyone so He will break out of any mold or box that we put Him in. Sometime, we structure Him out of our church programs and agendas and when He comes to bless us as we ask or petition Him to, He is not allowed in.

Once He showed me how He is not allowed in when He comes to us after we have cried out to Him in prayer to bless us. It happened one day during a prayer meeting that I attended. This prayer meeting was very structured and the elderly ladies leading it had been doing it for years. On this day while we were praying, an African American woman came in and she sat down and she immediately began to cry about her life, about where she was financially (no money and no home) and how she does not see a future for herself. Almost immediately, the leader of the prayer group asked that she be removed to another room because her crying was a disturbance and she was disrupting the prayer agenda for that day.

Because I love the voice of Lord and I am so aware of His voice, as soon as the woman opened her mouth and began to cry, I heard the voice of God the Father crying in this woman so I went to her and I placed my hand around her to comfort her. The leader of the prayer group turned to me and rebuked me. She said that I cannot comfort her in the prayer room and that she needed to be removed to another room. I tried to explain to her that God the Father was actually the one crying through the woman but she would not hear it and the woman was removed. As they were taking her away, God the Father began to wail and when He stopped He said to me, **"You see how I come to my people and they reject Me after they have cried to Me for revival and cried for Me to move in their midst? They cannot recognize Me when I do not come the way they want and know. I came in that woman crying to them to minister to Me but they would not. If they had ministered to Me in that woman, I would have released to them those things that they had petitioned Me for but instead, I was driven away."**

We all have to know the day of our visitation because God will come to us in the most unlikely person and sometimes in the most unlikely place. We must learn from the way the Jewish leaders (the Pharisees and the Sadducees) rejected the Lord because He was not one of their priests or from "a priestly lineage." They only saw Him as a Nazarene and a carpenter and nothing more. Also, the Lord Jesus said that whatsoever we do to the least of His brethren, we do it to Him. Only wisdom can help us walk in love and discernment.

3. Your Path Becomes a Shining Light:

Also, you will find that when divine wisdom begins to lead you, some people can be having a conversation and they may not know you and you may not even be a part of the conversation but you can hear God giving you instructions from their lips. They might not even be born again and as a result will not even know that they are speaking God's instruction to you. It is one of the awesome ways of the Lord because God can use anyone. All souls belong to Him and He can use them when He wants. This is why God can lead you no matter where you are as long as you are on the path of safety because He is the light in your path. It is the reason that **Proverbs 4:18** says that the path of the just is like the shinning light:

"But the path of the just is as the shining light, that shineth more and more unto the perfect day."

If there is any darkness that is coming against you, you want to know it before hand and you want to know why. For me, God forewarns me in many ways and one of those ways is by giving me a vision of black clouds moving towards me and I would immediately say, "Father, in the name of Jesus, I change these black clouds to white clouds of glory." The next thing that I do is send the black clouds back to the devil and I will command him to fall into the wickedness that he is planning against me. I will then speak to the white clouds to appear and be a blessing to me. I thank God for always letting me know when the devil is on the move against me. He lets me see as the white clouds replace the black.

If you are someone who waits for things to happen in the realm of the physical before you react, you will always be too late to respond to the devil's plans against you because you are waiting for things to manifest before you address them. But when you are in this path of safety, you will find that as God's friend and confidant, He will always show you what is about to happen so that you have an opportunity to determine the outcome. He gives you an opportunity to create your desired outcome by changing what happens in the realm of the spirit. He lets you have a say so in what takes place in your life so that you do not have to wait for unpleasant and evil things to happen and then begin to cry. For instance, if somebody is going to get sick in your family, you should be able to at least get a glimpse of what the devil is trying to do so that you will know how to pray or change the outcome. This is why we serve a Living God. He lets us know what is about to happen and He helps us to change the outcome to what we desire.

If you look at the ministry of the Lord Jesus, you will see that He knew the outcome of every situation that He was called to. When they told Him to come because Lazarus was sick, He told them that the sickness was not unto death and to prove His point, He spent three days doing something else before He finally decided to go and even then, He was in no hurry **(John 11:1-44)**. Also, when Jairus' daughter was sick and even at the point of death according to **Mark 5:35-42,** He again was in no hurry but told Jairus to only believe!

> **"While he yet spake, there came from the ruler of the synagogue's house certain which said, Thy daughter is dead: why troublest thou the Master any further?** *36* **As soon as Jesus heard the word that was spoken, he saith unto the ruler of the synagogue, <u>Be not afraid</u>, <u>only believe</u>"** (Mark 5:35-36).

Even when the Lord got to Jairus' house and people were crying because the little girl was dead, He said to them:

> **"And when he was come in, he saith unto them, <u>Why make ye this ado, and weep</u>? <u>the damsel is not dead, but sleepeth</u>.** *40* **And they laughed him to scorn. But when he had put them all out, he taketh the father and the mother of the damsel, and them that were with him, and entereth in**

where the damsel was lying. *41*And he took the damsel by the hand, and said unto her, Talitha cumi; which is, being interpreted, Damsel, I say unto thee, arise. 42 <u>And straightway the damsel arose</u>, <u>and walked</u>; for she was of the age of twelve years. And they were astonished with a great astonishment" (Mark 5:39-42).

You can see that the Lord was not moved by the circumstances that He was presented with because He had a divine guidance from the Holy Spirit and He knew that He had the ability to remove unpleasant circumstances.

Today, we that have the Holy Spirit are to actually walk as He did and have the confidence in knowing that we have the ability to change circumstances and destroy the devil's plans. Therefore, we have to develop intimacy with Him and stay in the path of safety. We are to be like David who cried out constantly to know God more and more. If you read the Psalm and especially Psalm 119, you will see that David was always crying out to the Lord saying, **"Lead me in the path of thy statutes, teach me thy statutes, give me understanding, establish thy Word unto thy servant, etc.,"** because he knew that when God is leading you and when God is guiding you, you will always win even if the whole world is against you.

4. You Can Change and Defeat the Enemy's Plans:

We all need to cry out to the Lord to lead us in this path of safety and to guide us because if we do not, we will always wonder why we have to deal with the devil's wickedness undetected and without the knowledge to change them. The devil is an equal opportunity afflicter and he can only operate where a person has an open door for him to. In the path of safety, you can see and cancel the devil's plans against you.

The Lord once gave me a vision of the devil. In this vision, he was only about four feet tall but he was on the street with an old shotgun that looked as if part of the long tip had been sawed off.

He had no particular target as he was shooting into every house on both sides of the street as he walked and he was totally deranged. From the look of things, it seems as if he had terrorized people so much that everyone was in their house with their doors and windows closed. People were hiding in fear and no one dared to be on the street. Therefore, whoever did not close their doors and windows or was found on the street became an instant victim.

> *From the look of things in this vision, I was on the street and I was totally oblivious to the danger that I was in as I was playing with something that looked like a soccer ball with my feet. Because I was looking down at the ball as I played, I did not know that I was coming face-to-face with the devil. When I looked up, it was too late for me to run anywhere and besides, everyone seemed to have closed the doors to their house so that I had no place to run to even if I had the chance. At first, he was shocked that someone dared to walk the street that he was on and I saw him as he aimed his shotgun for a good shot at me. As I looked at him, I knew that I was in serious danger and right before he could fire his shotgun, a beautiful bride in her white wedding dress appeared from nowhere and stood over me covering me with her wedding gown. I saw the fear in the devil's eyes at the sight of this bride and he took off.*
>
> *As he was walking away, the scene changed because I was now part of a truck load of the Lord's soldiers assigned to patrol the streets. Our truck came up from behind him and we all jumped down from the truck and I was the first to get to him because of what he tried to do to me. I grabbed him from behind, lifted him up on my knee and broke him into two and his shotgun fell down and we rode off in victory.*

I know that the Lord has defeated the devil for me and I am purposed to walk in the victory and to change the devil's plans against me. It is true that I went through circumstances and even physical death that the devil thought were my final fate but I have seen God deliver me over and over again. He told me that the devil will forever be sorry that he rose up against me the way he did and I believe it and I walk accordingly. I no longer walk in the fear of the devil or his demons because I am in God's path of safety where the devil is blind concerning me.

Therefore, I say to you that whoever is not under cover takes a hit from the devil but when you are in the path of safety, you are safe because God covers you. The devil is not all-knowing and he does not know what goes on in your life until you either speak it (words, even whispers are spiritual broadcast in the spirit realm) or he is alerted to your activities when a "monitoring spirit" or a spirit of jealousy that is in someone around you reports to the next level of demons about your potential prosperity.

The devil's networks of demons have reporters in people to let them know when something good is about to happen to those around them. The evil spirits in the people will say to the next level of demons, "Guess who is trying to prosper; guess who is trying to come into something good?" The demons will pass the message on and the next thing you know is that the thing is attacked and you loose it. This happens sometimes, when someone goes for a job interview and they know that they are about to get the job and they get on the phone and share it with a relative or friend and the next thing you know is that they loose that prospect.

That is why on the path of safety, the Lord begins to teach you how to use wisdom by zipping your mouth and how to know when to speak about what He is doing in your life because some of us talk too much. You meet some people and in five minuets they have told you the story of their lives and there is nothing left to hide. You should always ask the Lord what to share. Sometimes, I see things in the realm of the spirit about people but I no longer run to tell about them anymore. When God shows me something now, I pray and then if it is something that He wants me to go and speak to the person, I will go and share it and if I do not hear instruction to tell the person, I just pray for the person and ask the Lord to destroy the devil's plans against the person. I am no longer presumptuous in running to people with what I saw in the realm of the spirit because I have learned to be restrained and led by the Holy Spirit. I have also learned that when God wants to address an issue in someone's life, God initiates the process.

5. Evil Reports Will Not Move You:

When you are on the path of safety, you will find that as you go to places to minister, you will come out without affliction and you will not be worried about where you are going to minister. I have had some ministers say to me, "I went somewhere to minister about a year ago and I have been battling ... as a result." It should not be the case that you get afflicted when you go to a place to minister no matter the level of demonic activities in the place. You should not be afraid of going to foreign countries to minister and you should not allow people to use their past experiences to scare. What you need is to make sure that you are in God's secret place where the devil cannot touch you. I remember talking to someone about my intended trip to Kenya in Africa to minister and the conversation was just two weeks before my departure. The person said to me, "Oh, you had better pray before going to Africa because you do not want to come back dead." She then proceeded to tell me about someone she knew who went to Africa and came back sick but she recovered. When the person went back the second time, she got sick again and died.

That was what someone told me two weeks before my departure to Kenya and I thought that was some kind of encouragement. I said, "Satan, get behind me because the Bible says that no weapon formed against me shall prosper. Therefore, I will go on the journey in peace and come back safely." God knows the path that has serpents and scorpions and Jesus gave us "authority to tread upon serpents and scorpions." We do not have to fear devils because the Lord has already given us power to tread upon them.

Once you begin to let the Word of God transform your mind and avoid sins and iniquities, you will see that because you are on this path of safety, you will not be afraid even if the devil was to walk into your bedroom. You will realize that you have power over him and that he is like nothing.

As a newly born again Christian, I used to be afraid of the devil but God in His wisdom allowed him to come against me so many times and in so many ways that I lost my fear of him. I used to be terrified when he would show up on my job, in a person physically or just walk into my bedroom but after my numerous encounters with him, I found out that by God's grace, the fear was gone because having encounters with him and rebuking him was God's chosen way to help me loose the fear. One day, he came into my bedroom raging and puffing against me and I said to him, "Excuse me, how long have you been on this job now? You have been on this job before Adam was created and do you know when I got born again? 1992 and I am kicking your butt. You are not very good at this job." Since then, he does not come around me anymore because he hates to be disgraced or put in his place.

There is a class of holy angels that I see, and I would know that the devil himself is trying to make a move towards me. Give it one, two or three days and satan himself is on the scene. God has assigned a class of angels to protect us from satan. Also, when I see a particular class of wicked angels, it also means that satan himself is not far behind them. God allows me to see these types of angels because He does not want them to surprise me but it is my duty to stay on the path of safety.

6. You Will Know the Benefits of Dying to Self:
Once the Lord told me that He wants me to place myself on the cross of dying to self because when I am on the cross of dying to myself, all I can do is look down at the people persecuting me. From the cross, I can see the true state of people and it will cause love and compassion to rise up within me so that I can look up to Him as my Father and cry, "Father, forgive them for they know not what they

do." This enables God to move on my behalf. He raised up the Lord on the third day. Therefore, we must be assured that there is nothing happening in our lives that He cannot get us out of. As long as you are your own avenger, you leave no room for God to operate so we must purpose to search out this path of safety and we need to stay on it. It is a path of dying to self.

I love what Derek Prince said. According to him, "When we get born again, God does not preach to our 'old man' (our sinful and rebellious nature) nor does He try to conform or convert him. He has only one solution for our old man —execution!" God crucifies our old rebellious nature (flesh) because the Bible tells us that the carnal mind is at enmity against God. As long as you are carnal, as long as you are not dying to your flesh and becoming transformed by the Word of God, and as long as your mind is not being renewed by the Word of God, you at enmity in your mind against God. You will immediately judge God when things do not go your way, when you do not understand what is going on in your life or when you are in a spiritual trial.

Also, when the Word of God comes to you, your mind will tell you that it does not make sense or that you know better and your mind will help you to circumvent what was said to you by the Word of God that came to you. As a result, you will do your own thing —iniquity and cannot see anything wrong with what you did. Without knowing, you go through life as the Lord of your own life. But, on the path of safety, you truly have to make Jesus the Lord of your life and the Lord of your circumstances. He will begin to work in you both to will and to do of His good pleasure. As I said before, our actions are controlled by our thoughts and wrong thinking produces wrong or bad actions.

I discovered that God actually takes pleasure in us being a people or vessels that He can work through and He enjoys showing us off. Sometimes, I see Him and He has a mantle like the one on a fireplace and depending on what the nature of the assignment is; He would display the corresponding item on it. Sometimes, it is a beautiful serving dish, a beautiful teacup, a serving platter or a beautiful vase. There are times that it is a spoon, a mug, a water jug, etc. I have seen Him take a very beautiful mug that He has taken the time to design and put it back in the fire because He wants to refine it some more. When I see this, it means that I should get ready for the refiner's fire because there is something He does not like and He wants to remove it from my life. Yes, I will go through a trial or adverse situation but He will get the job done because He wants me to hold more of the glory that He has for me and He wants it to overflow through me.

7. Prayer to Ask the Lord to Set You on the Path of Safety: You have to petition God to place you on the path of safety as you change your ways to His and rely on the leading of His Spirit. I believe that the prayer below will help you to petition the Lord when you pray it sincerely and in faith. The Lord will set you on the path of safety, for wisdom to lead you and for the grace to die to yourself so that His plans can come to pass in your life.

"Father, in the name of the Lord Jesus, I thank You for Your Word. I thank You that it is Your will for me to dwell underneath the shadow of Your wings, to walk in this path that the evil birds do not walk in and that the lions, the scorpions, and the serpents cannot come into

"Father, I thank You that when I come upon serpents and scorpions, I tread upon them with Your power and authority and nothing shall by any means hurt me. Thank You that You have become an enemy to my enemies, You avenge me, You defend and protect me. Father, I cry now in the name of the Lord Jesus, that You set me on this path and Father, that You will give me the grace to walk in this path without wavering. I choose this path of safety for all the days of my life and I ask that You guide me with Your eye and let Your wisdom will lead me as I walk in this path.

> *"Father God, in the name of the Lord Jesus, I repent for not being on the path before this time; not being where You could have protected me from the things that I had gone through that were not Your will for me but today in the name of Jesus, I purpose to walk in this path that the evil birds cannot see into, that the lions cannot walk in and that is a path of holiness. Forever I choose this highway of holiness and I thank You for Your wisdom that now leads me and for Your grace upon me forever. I purpose to die to my own flesh and my own desire and I say, 'Lord, not my will but Your will be done in my life and through me all the days of my life forever in Jesus name. Amen.'"*

Note: *If you are sitting, please stand up and take a step forward into the path of safety.*

Seven Things that Will Keep You in the Path of Safety:

I have a summary of the seven things that you need to learn that will keep you in the path of safety. They are:

1. Walk in Meekness:

Meekness is the first requirement for remaining in this path so you want to learn to walk in meekness.

> "<u>**The meek will he guide in judgment**</u>: <u>**and the meek will he teach his way**</u>. *10* **All the paths of the LORD are mercy and truth unto such as keep his covenant and his testimonies. *11* For thy name's sake, O LORD, pardon mine iniquity; for it is great. *12* What man is he that feareth the LORD? him shall he teach in the way that he shall choose. *13* His soul shall dwell at ease; and his seed shall inherit the earth. *14* The secret of the LORD is with them that fear him; and he will shew them his covenant.**"

You must walk in meekness and choose righteousness everyday of your life.

2. Walk in Love and Be a Covenant Keeper:

The Bible tells us that love never fails. It is the greatest weapon on planet earth and there is no law that says that you are to hate another person rather than love them. Our God is love and that makes us children of love. You must walk in love in order to stay on the path of safety.

Also, you must also be a covenant keeper if you want to stay on the path of safety. This means that you must be a person of your word. Do not make a promise to someone and just because some other person offered you something that is better for you, you just drop the first person and go with the second offer. When you do this, you are a covenant breaker and are not qualified to be in the path of safety. Our God is the God that keeps covenant. If you look at the pains that we human beings have brought Him, you will be amazed that He is still willing to be part of our lives. One of the reasons that He puts up with us is because of His covenant through the blood of His Son, Jesus Christ. We must walk like Him when it comes to covenants.

3. Have Integrity:

Keeping the Word of the Lord and keeping your word go hand in hand with keeping covenants because sometimes, there might not be a covenant but the Word of God in your life and how well you keep your word—integrity! The Lord once told me that, "A person is only as good as his or her word." If your word is worth nothing because you never keep your word, then God will have a hard time using you no matter how anointed you are. As I stated before, He said that those who do not keep their words will only make Him look bad if He should release them to do things for Him the way they ask Him to. Therefore, be a person of your word. If you promise to show up for something, then by all means show up for it or else, God cannot trust you.

4. Keep Thy Lips from Speaking Guile:

The things that we say can either bring us a blessing or a curse. Therefore, we must be careful not to open doors to the devil in our lives with what we say. The Word of the Lord says in **Psalm 34:12-16:**

> "**What man is he that desireth life**, and **loveth many days, that he may see good? Keep thy tongue from evil**, and **thy lips from speaking guile**. Depart from evil, and do good; seek peace, and pursue it. The eyes of the LORD are upon the righteous, and his ears are open unto their cry. The face of the LORD is against them that do evil, to cut off the remembrance of them from the earth."

Also, **Proverbs 15:4** says:

> "**A wholesome tongue is a tree of life**: but perverseness therein is a breach in the spirit."

Proverbs 18:21 says:

> "**Death and life are in the power of the tongue**: and they that love it shall eat the fruit thereof."

The tongue can easily keep you from walking in the path of safety. **James 3:5-9** also tells us that the tongue can lead to hell so we have to be careful of what we say and how we say it.

> "**Even so the tongue is a little member, and boasteth great things**. Behold, **how great a matter a little fire kindleth!** *6* And **the tongue is a fire, a world of iniquity: so is the tongue among our members**, that **it defileth the whole body, and setteth on fire the course of nature**; and **it is set on fire of hell**. *7* For every kind of beasts, and of birds, and of serpents, and of things in the sea, is

tamed, and hath been tamed of mankind: *8* **But the tongue can no man tame; it is an unruly evil, full of deadly poison.** *9* **Therewith bless we God, even the Father; and therewith curse we men,** which are made after the similitude of God."

5. **Depart from Evil and Do Good:**
To stay on the path of safety, you must choose to depart from evil and do good. You must also be someone who seeks peace and pursues it. These are the nuggets that the Lord Jesus was giving us in the Sermon on the Mount when He said, **"Love your enemies, do good to those that hate you, bless those who persecute you and pray for those who despitefully use you."** When you are doing these things guess who becomes your shield and your avenger? God Himself! God avenges you Himself because He is the defender of the oppressed.

If you leave enough room for Him, He will defend you. As I shared with you earlier on in this chapter under the subtitle of *Understanding the Need for Holiness*, I was judged for speaking against my sister who lives in Nigeria. When I took the fall, my sister did not even know that God was fighting on her behalf. God defended her by making sure that I knew never to touch her again that way.

6. **Avoid Iniquities and Walk in the Fear of the Lord:**
God hates iniquities and we are to hate acts of iniquities also. **Psalm 107:17** says:

"**Fools because of their transgression, and because of their iniquities, are afflicted.**"

And also **Psalm 25:11** says:

"**For thy name's sake, O LORD, pardon mine iniquity; for it is great.**"

The fear of the Lord must be in every believer and we must fear God enough to avoid iniquities. This is not taught much in the church today because some people do not think that you need to fear God. They think that because the Bible says that God is love, we do not have to fear Him but I say to you again that the Lord Jesus taught us that there is only one person that we need to fear –God! **"But I will forewarn you whom ye shall fear: Fear him, which after he hath killed hath power to cast into hell; yea, I say unto you, Fear him"** (Luke 12:5). Yes, God alone has the power to cast someone into hell if the person lived his or her life in iniquities and sin.

Because a lot of people do not walk very closely with God and have not seen God, they think it is not right to say that we have to fear God. It is true that God is merciful and God forgives but He is also the Highest Judge and He will by no means acquit the guilty. Yes, this loving God will one day send some people to hell for their sins. I told you before that the fact that David was a man after God's heart did not keep God from pronouncing a serious judgment on David when he killed Uriah.

One of the things that you will discover about God as you walk closely with Him is that God can thunder at you. When you do something that He knows He has taught you not to do or when you insist on having your way, God can come down on you like a thunder! I mean that He will thunder on you and there is no hiding place for you and there is no where for you to run. Twice I have seen Him thunder and it was awe inspiring and dreadful. Once He thundered at me as He declared, "Because I Am!" It was His reaction to one of my foolish thoughts. All I had was a thought that challenged His ways and His question to me was, "Who do you think you are?" He is the I AM THAT I AM and we must all remember Him as such and His fear must be in us enough to keep us from evil.

God is our friend and He is also a judge and He hates sin. His Word does not change and according to Him, the souls that sin must die. In other words, if you continue in a life of sin and your Christianity is nothing but a lip service to Him, He says that you are a hypocrite and if you die in your sins, He will send you to hell. Therefore, you have to fear Him enough to want to do right, live righteously and live holy. It says in **Psalm 34:15-16:**

> "**The eyes of the LORD are upon the righteous, and his ears are open unto their cry.** *16* <u>**The face of the LORD is against them that do evil, to cut off the remembrance of them from the earth.**</u>"

The Lord Jesus said in **Luke 13:27** that He will say to the workers of iniquities at the final judgment to get away from Him. He will drive them away from His presence and His heaven forever:

> "**But he shall say, I tell you, I know you not whence ye are;** <u>**depart from me, all ye workers of iniquity.**</u>"

God will judge all workers of iniquities and He does not allow them to walk on the path of safety. If you are in this path of safety, you avoid iniquities and you pursue righteousness, God will protect you. Remember that He said in **Psalm 32:8** that He will instruct you and guide you with His eye:

> "<u>**I will instruct thee and teach thee in the way which thou shalt go:**</u> <u>**I will guide thee with mine eye.**</u>"

He is talking about the Holy Spirit; He becomes your guide. He will wake you up when you need to wake up and He will let you know what you are to do or not to do. This is wonderful because sometimes I forget to review my morning appointments and I go to bed thinking that I have a free morning but the Lord will tell me to get up, take a shower and go to the office. I will get there and within five minuets or so, someone would arrive for their morning appointment with me.

The following scriptures tell us more of the promises that God made to those who walk closely with Him. **Proverbs 16:7** says:

> "**When a man's ways please the LORD, he maketh even his enemies to be at peace with him.**"

Also, **Psalm 31:20** says:

> "**Thou shalt hide them in the secret of thy presence** from the pride of man: **thou shalt keep them secretly in a pavilion** from the strife of tongues."

Also, He promised in **Isaiah 26:3** to keep those who set their mind on Him in perfect peace.

> "Thou wilt keep him in perfect peace, whose mind is stayed on thee: because he trusteth in thee."

He knows how your day is going to be and He protects you from the evil tongue and from wicked men and women. I like the scripture in **Deuteronomy 33:27** that says:

> "The eternal God is thy refuge, and underneath are the everlasting arms: and he shall thrust out the enemy from before thee; and shall say, Destroy them."

In other words, God sees to it that **"As your days, so shall your strength be"** (Deuteronomy 33:25 ESV). He helps you to organize your day so that it is not a "yoyo." Some people have good and bad days but God wants to normalize your days so that they do not fluctuate between good and bad. I usually tell people that I do not have a bad or a good day because all my days are blessed. If I have an issue or circumstance to deal with, I deal with it and I move on but I will not let it affect the rest of the day.

For instance, the day that my dad died, I was at a Benny Hinn's crusade because God woke me up that morning saying, "You shall receive of the fullness of His (Jesus) grace" so I knew that God had something to give me that day. I also knew that I was to go to Benny Hinn's crusade. Throughout the time that Benny Hinn ministered, nothing out of the ordinary happened for me but at the end of the evening when he said, "Good night everybody," I saw virtue (the anointing) coming from him and making a beeline for me and it landed on me and I was drunk in the Spirit instantly! I was at the very back of the dome but that anointing found me and landed on me but I had no idea what I was going home to confront.

I got home drunk and made my way to the bedroom but I thought it was strange for my brother to be sitting in the living room with so many people at 2 am and no one was saying a word. Then my brother came in and broke the news to me in anger. He said, "Where have you been? We have been looking for you because your dad is dead!" I was so drunk in the spirit that all I could say was praise the Lord. I turned to the Lord and I said, "Lord is my dad with You?" He said, "Yes" and I said ok and went to bed. My brother must have though that I was strange because all his friends were in the living room consoling him through the night and throughout the next day but I did not cry. Once I found out that he was with the Lord, I went to bed and I woke up and went to church.

On the way home from church, it finally hit me that my dad was gone and I said, "Oh Lord, my dad is dead" and He said, "Yes, but he is with Me." Although I do not indulge in sweets much, I will occasionally buy the smallest cup of vanilla ice cream when I feel like I need to celebrate and the Lord knows this so He said to me, "Go buy yourself an ice cream." So, I pulled into a store and I bought a cup of ice cream and I got home and my brother was still being consoled by some of his friends and I said to him, "do you want some ice cream?" He said, "Yes" and we ate the ice cream. The Lord wanted me to celebrate the fact that my dad was with Him. Some people take years to recover after the death of their parents but the anointing the Lord gave me that night was so strong that it acted as a buffer against the bad news of my dad's death. Truly, God will anoint you to handle each day of your life if you let Him.

I did not have to cry because of my dad's death or because I did not know where he went (heaven or hell) because the Lord was with me and comforted me. Walking closely with the Lord enables the Lord to protect us and make sure that we do not walk in ignorance. There are some people that go through things and they do not have a clue as to why they went through it. When you are in the secret place with the Lord, if something happens that is unpleasant, you want to pull yourself aside to the Lord and ask Him about why it happened and what you are to do about it. The Lord will help you walk through it and He will deliver you. You will also begin to see that Wisdom is a teacher and She will begin to show you how God's principles are laid out, what spiritual principles you need to operate and what spiritual principles will work against you if you violate them or operate them ignorantly.

7. Let the Lord Be Your Light:

For the purpose of this discussion, the last thing that will keep you on the path of safety is found in two scriptures. The first one is in **Psalm 27:1-6**. You must pursue God with all your heart and desire Him above all else.

> "**The LORD is my light and my salvation; whom shall I fear**? the LORD is the strength of my life; of whom shall I be afraid? *2* **When the wicked, even mine enemies and my foes, came upon me to eat up my flesh, they stumbled and fell. *3* Though an host should encamp against me, my heart shall not fear: though war should rise against me, in this will I be confident. *4* One thing have I desired of the LORD, that will I seek after**; that I may dwell in the house of the LORD all the days of my life, to behold the beauty of the LORD, and to enquire in his temple. *5* **For in the time of trouble he shall hide me in his pavilion: in the secret of his tabernacle shall he hide me**; he shall set me up upon a rock. *6* And now shall mine head be lifted up above mine enemies round about me: therefore will I offer in his tabernacle sacrifices of joy; I will sing, yea, I will sing praises unto the LORD."

When you are on this path, the Lord lights your path and He makes sure that nothing surprises you but you must be one who seeks after the Lord with all your heart. Just as Tommy Tenney said, you must be *"A God Chaser."* When you pursue God with all your heart, you will find that your love for Him intensifies and you will want to do things that please Him. No one has to preach to you to do right or avoid sin because you are now aiming to please God and not man. Some time ago, I went to Him and I felt that maybe He would make an exception for me because we are kind tight. I said to Him, "Father, I want to do…and He said, "Really?" and I said, "Yes." Then He asked me, "But, how will that glorify Me?" This is one of those instances that He lets you think about your request. He then asked me if I had purposed to do everything to the praise and glory of His name and I said yes. I got the point that He was making and I know that He wants us to succeed in our endeavors. He is not our enemy but our Father and Friend and He knows when we are struggling with things that our flesh really desire. He will lovingly let you know that you cannot do that anymore.

A few months ago, some lady came into my office and she informed me that she was pregnant and that she has made up her mind not to have the baby. According to her, she was going to have an abortion and she would repent afterwards. I asked her if she had read the Word of God about those who crucify the Lord a second time. I talked and talked to her about the consequences of willful sin but she would not listen and sure enough, she had the abortion. When I found out that she went through with her decision, I said, "Well, I have done my part." I gave her the Word of God and she has a right to exercise her free will. No one can take that away from her so I let it go. Not long after, she called me up all laughing and elated as though nothing had happened and she wanted me to act as though everything was fine. I knew that I was dealing with someone who has no fear of the Lord and who has no clue about the nature of the God she is dealing with.

A person who continues in the path of willful sin cannot walk in the path of safety and when they die, they will have to face God as their judge and they will not like what He will say to them at that time. I say to you again that the Lord Jesus said a day is coming in which He will say to some people, **"I never knew you: <u>depart</u>**

from me, ye that work iniquity." Iniquity is setting aside the Word of God and doing your own thing.

The Bible says in **Galatians 6:7** that God is not mocked and that whatsoever a man sows, that shall he also reap. If you do an act of evil willfully with the intention to repent afterwards, God knows it and He also knows how to deal with you. The grace of God covers us when we are ignorant but when we do evil willfully and purposefully with the intention to repent afterwards and we know the Word and are in church, then God will judge us for our actions. It is called an abuse or despise of the Spirit of Grace in **Hebrews 6:4-6:**

> "**For it is impossible for those who were once enlightened, and have tasted of the heavenly gift,** and were made partakers of the Holy Ghost, *5* And have tasted the good word of God, and the powers of the world to come, *6* If they shall fall away, **to renew them again unto repentance; seeing they crucify to themselves the Son of God afresh**, and **put him to an open shame**."

Hebrews 10:29 also says:

> "**Of how much sorer punishment**, suppose ye, **shall he be thought worthy, who hath trodden under foot the Son of God**, and hath counted the blood of the covenant, wherewith he was sanctified, an unholy thing, and **hath done despite unto the Spirit of grace**?"

I thank God that we are in the days of grace because if it was under the Old Covenant, God's judgment would come upon her instantly or she would have been stoned to death because according to the Law, if you do the crime, you pay the price.

Our last scripture in helping us stay on the path of safety is in **Psalm 28:7:**

> **"The LORD is my strength and my shield; my heart trusted in him, and I am helped: therefore my heart greatly rejoiceth; and with my song will I praise him."**

When you learn to make the Lord your strength and your shield and stop defending yourself, stop trying to make those who are speaking against you to stop, and just walk in love, righteousness, holiness and forgiveness, God becomes your strength and your shield and He rises up to defend you. Human beings are very fickle in their ways. The same people who are saying crucify you today will be hailing you tomorrow when God raises you for His glory. As a test of human fickleness all you have to do is just become someone rich, great or famous and many of them will be related to you and all of them will begin to claim to know you. They will be telling people how they used to be your friend and they will forget that they used to speak against you. This is why the Bible says that, **"The poor is hated even of his own neighbour: but the rich hath many friends"** (Proverbs 14:20). People are not quick to claim a poor man as their relative but everyone wants to be related to a rich man. Therefore, allow the Lord to make you the person He created you to be and do not pay attention to your critics.

The path of safety is a path of dying to self, therefore do not try to defend yourself but let the Lord be your shield. Remember that I said before that according to the book of Isaiah, the ravenous birds or vultures, fierce lions, etc., will not be found on the path of safety because only the redeemed of the Lord will walk in it. At the end, it says that they shall come with joy and singing and everlasting joy shall be upon their heads because when you are in this path, God sees to it that no matter what you are going through the joy of the Lord is your strength. You need to set aside time to really study the scriptures in this chapter for yourself; to really apprehend the Lord and this path of safety in your life where you are guaranteed protection, provisions and promotion. You will actually be walking in the place where the devil's fiery darts will just drop off and not touch you. When tongues rise up against you, the words that used to pierce you and make you cry will no longer have any effect on you.

Conclusion

Having read this book, you can see for yourself that covenants have power and that we cannot just ignore them in our lives. **A covenant is a binding agreement both spiritually and physically and the covenants in our lives impact us for good or for bad on a daily basis. We all make covenants knowingly and unknowingly with our words, promises, oaths, vows, actions, places we visit, etc.** Therefore, we must make efforts to understand them, to know how God uses them and also how the devil uses them. Doing this, will help us to know what we are to do when someone wants to bring us into a covenant agreement with them. We can stop and ask ourselves about the impact that making the covenant will have on our lives. Will making the covenant be in line with the New Covenant that we have with God the Father through His Son, Jesus Christ? Will making the covenant bring us a blessing or a curse? Will it open the door for the devil to begin to afflict us and other members of our families?

A proposition for a covenant agreement could come as a simple request from one of your pals asking or inviting you to visit his or her place or for you to give or receive something from him or her. If the person is into things that are ungodly or the place you are being invited to is an ungodly place and you say yes to the request, you have a covenant that the devil can later use against you whenever he wants. It matters who you associate with. Therefore, we must ask ourselves the critical questions above before coming into a covenant agreement with anyone in our personal life, in the workplace, in our business and in our Christian life.

We also need to learn how to correctly apply the covenant that we have with the Lord. I showed you in this book the Lord Jesus' reactions whenever someone invoked the wrong covenant or incorrectly applied a covenant when dealing with Him. He would go silent because He knows that the person does not know how to use covenant. He went silent in **Matthew 15:21-28** when the Canaanite woman invoked the wrong covenant while she was asking Him to heal her daughter that was possessed with a devil. He could not help her under the covenant that she invoked because she was not covered by the covenant. That covenant was meant only for the children of Israel.

He again became silent when the Pharisees and the Sadducees also invoked the covenant of the Law when they brought the woman that was caught in adultery. He was sent by God the Father to bring them the New Covenant of grace and mercy but they missed what God had for them in Him by their lack of understanding. They were holding on to the old covenant while He was offering them a new covenant. We are to learn from their mistakes by understanding the nature of the covenant that we have with the Lord and we are to know how God wants us to use the covenant in order to get the results that He has for us.

We must also know what God promised to do for us under this covenant and what He expects us to do under the terms of our covenant with Him. Under the new covenant that the Lord established with His blood, God has certain duties and we the believers have certain duties. We cannot petition God to do for us what He has already commanded us to do neither should we be spending hours asking Him to do what He has already freely promised to do. This means that we need to learn how to operate the covenant His way so that we can have the results that He has already freely given us in Christ.

It is my belief that those who do not understand the power of covenant will abuse the covenants in their lives and will not be effective in apprehending the things that God has for them. They will also ignorantly open doors for the devil to work against them and their loved ones. Therefore, to avoid the devil using covenant agreements to hinder you, you need to understand covenants and how he uses them so that you can beat him at his game. **You also need to know what covenants have been working against you in your family or what covenants have been at work in the family that you married into.** You can marry a person without marrying into the ungodly covenants in his or her family. You need to remove the ungodly covenants in your life so that you can be successful in life.

As long as evil covenants are in place and intact in your life, the devil will always be able to come into your life to set you back, cause havoc in your family relationships or in your children and destroy what you are trying to build. Our God is a covenant keeping God and if you make a covenant with the devil, that covenant will remain in place and God cannot move on your behalf because He honors covenants. As I stated in this book, the covenant that Adam made with the devil on behalf of all mankind is still in effect in the life of every unbeliever today. A person is only free from this Adamic Covenant when the person of his or her own free will chooses the covenant that the Lord Jesus established with His own blood.

Yes, covenants have power. You can see the negative effects of ungodly covenants such as poverty, unmarriedness, divorce, rape, theft, imprisonment, idleness, failure, premature death, murder, sickness and diseases in some families. Each generation in these families have to deal with these issues because of the ungodly covenants that are still intact in their lives. Until someone rises up in these families to remove them, the family members will continue to suffer the negative consequences of the covenants.

You must also learn how to walk in the path of safety where the devil is powerless against you and your endeavors. You need divine grace and wisdom to stay on this path. Therefore, I encourage you to read and re-read this book because it will show you how to be set free and how to set your family members free from evil covenants. It will help to make your prayers become more effective as you begin to correctly use the covenant that we have with the Lord. May God bless you.

Bibliography

Ogenaarekhua, Mary J. *How to Discern and Expel Evil Spirits.* Atlanta, GA: To His Glory Publishing, Inc., 2005.

Ogenaarekhua, Mary J. *Keys to Understanding Your Visions and Dreams.* Atlanta, GA: To His Glory Publishing, Inc., 2004.

Ogenaarekhua, Mary J. A *Teacher's Manual on Visions and Dreams.* Atlanta, GA: To His Glory Publishing, Inc., 2004.

To His Glory Publishing

Let Us Publish Your Book

To His Glory Publishing Company will publish your book at the least expensive cost. We pay one of the highest royalties in the industry – 40%! We print on demand and place your book on the major online bookstores such a Amazon.com, Barnesandnoble.com, Bookamillion.com, etc.

  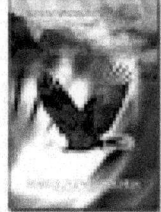  

WWW.TOHISGLORYPUBLISHING.COM
(770) 458-7947

TO HIS GLORY PUBLISHING COMPANY, INC.

463 Dogwood Dr. Lilburn, GA. 30047, U.S.A (770)458-7947

Order Form for Bookstores in the USA

Order Date: _____
Order Placed By: _____   By Fax: _____
Address: _____

City _____ ST/ZIP _____
Phone #:
Email: _____
Purchase Order#: _____

Return Policy: Within 1 year but not before 90 Days.

Price	Quantity	List Price
Shipping Method:		
Media:		
UPS:		
FedEx:		
Other (Please Secify):		
Total Price:	**Total Quantity:**	**List Price**

Ship To Address: **Bill to Address:**

TO HIS GLORY PUBLISHING COMPANY, INC. • 463 Dogwood Dr. Lilburn, GA. 30047, U.S.A (770)458-7947

www.ingramcontent.com/pod-product-compliance
Lightning Source LLC
Chambersburg PA
CBHW061305110426
42742CB00012BA/2066